CRADDOCK STORIES

"*When I was in my late teens, I wanted to be a preacher. When I was in my late twenties, I wanted to be a good preacher. Now that I am older, I want more than anything else to be a Christian. To live simply, to love generously, to speak truthfully, to serve faithfully, and leave everything else to God.*"

–Fred B. Craddock

CRADDOCK STORIES

By Fred B. Craddock

Edited by Mike Graves and
Richard F. Ward

CHALICE
PRESS

ST. LOUIS, MISSOURI

The publishers have generously given permission to use extended quotations from the following works by Fred B. Craddock:

"Praying Through Clenched Teeth." In *The Twentieth Century Pulpit,* vol. 2. Edited by James W. Cox. Nashville: Abingdon Press, 1981.

Overhearing the Gospel. Nashville: Abingdon Press, 1978.

As One Without Authority. St. Louis: Chalice Press, 2001.

"On Being Pentecostal." In *Best Sermons 1.* Edited by James W. Cox. San Francisco: Harper and Row, 1988.

"Have You Ever Heard John Preach?" In *Best Sermons 4.* Edited by James W. Cox. New York: HarperCollins, 1991.

Cover photo: © Nancy Anne Dawe
Cover design: Lynne Condellone
Interior design: Elizabeth Wright
Interior photo: Bill Mahan, Cherry Log Christian Church
Art direction: Michael Domínguez

Visit Chalice Press on the World Wide Web at
www.chalicepress.com

10 9 8 7 6 5   05 06 07 08 09 10

Library of Congress Cataloging–in–Publication Data

Craddock, Fred B.
   Craddock stories / by Fred B. Craddock ; edited by Mike Graves and Richard F. Ward.
      p.   cm.
   ISBN-10: 0-827204-83-3
   ISBN-13: 978-0-827204-83-6
   (pbk. : alk. paper)
   1. Story sermons.   2. Sermons, American.   I. Graves, Mike. II. Ward, Richard F. III. Title.
   BV4307.S7 C73   2001
   252'.0663--dc21   2001000777

Printed in the United States of America

For the ministries of
Fred and Nettie Craddock,
εὐχαριστοῦμεν

Contents

Acknowledgments

It has been said that some things are too important to do alone, like church, for instance. Of course, some projects are too big to do alone, like this collection. Therefore, we wish to thank the following: Jon L. Berquist, for his patient and perceptive editorial eye; our graduate assistants, especially Nicole Finkelstein-Blair and A. J. Ballou, who transcribed hours upon hours of Fred Craddock's sermons; the various churches, seminary librarians, and regional offices of the Christian Church (Disciples of Christ) for all their help in securing tapes of sermons; our families, who encouraged us along the way; the faith and learning communities of Central Baptist Theological Seminary in Kansas City and Iliff School of Theology in Denver, who support us; George Nikas and Marilyn Schertz of CST Media; and the saints of the Cherry Log Christian Church (Disciples of Christ), who so graciously welcomed us into their community of faith.

Introduction

There is a preacher I know who has a clay figurine called "Pueblo Storyteller" in her study. You may have seen this figure before, as it is quite prolific these days. "Pueblo Storyteller" is showing up in homes everywhere, near fireplaces, in living rooms, libraries, dens, and on mantles. He is the creation of Helen Cordero, a Native American potter of the Cochita Pueblos who, in 1964, wanted to honor the memory of her grandfather. Known among the Cochitas as a gifted storyteller, Santiago Quintana wanted the traditions of his people preserved, especially in the memories of the children. "Come children, it is time!" And the children would gather around him to listen to his stories of the people, Cordero remembers.

She has captured this image in clay and painted it in the colors of earth and sky. The Storyteller's eyes are closed, but the mouth is opened to a round "O". His eyes are closed because all storytellers have to keep a steady gaze on their inner worlds of memory, perception, and imagination; his mouth is open in order to transport others through the medium of sound, language, and imagery. Children are attached to the Storyteller in various places and exhibit a variety of emotional attitudes and facial expressions—one is crying in the cradle of his arm; one is sleeping in his lap; one is climbing to the top of his head; and another is listening peacefully on his knee.

We, of course, could be any one of them. Or we could sit in the Storyteller's place. As preachers of the gospel of Jesus Christ, we are entrusted with stories others have been telling for ages and will be telling for ages to come. Do we attach ourselves to these gospel stories, or have they attached themselves to us? No matter. In either case, we sit in those holy spaces they create, and there we laugh, weep, rest, or remain restless.

We also look deeply into our own hearts in order to tell our stories of faith—to give an account of those places where we too have encountered the living Christ. This is why Fred Craddock has been the "Storyteller" for many of us. We cling to the stories he tells, not simply because they comfort us, make us laugh or cry, or leave us scratching our heads. We cling to them because we hear in them both dissonance and harmony between our stories and the stories of God.

It is not surprising that the "Pueblo Storyteller" sits very close to the Craddock books on this preacher's shelf. We certainly know Fred as a teacher of preachers. Fred opened the door to "inductive" preaching for a generation of preachers and revived the work of many who had been preaching for a long time. This method of preaching changed many preachers' thoughts about the ways that narrative material is brought into the service of the sermon. Simply put, an inductive method of preaching starts in the middle of human experience and moves from there to conclusions about the gospel. It is counterpoint to another method of preaching, "deductive," which states a truth in the form of a general proposition or conclusion, then breaks it down into points, instructions, and conclusions. In deductive preaching, stories and anecdotes are brought into service in the sermon to illustrate the points, little adornments that help dress the sermon up for church. Fred shows us that stories have a different sort of work to do in proclamation. What we experience in Fred's stories is the revelatory power of the gospel even while its wisdom remains hidden from the world.

Fred's homiletic has proven to be a capstone in the homiletical household for more than three decades. Even so, a good many preachers and other folk scratch their heads and say, "Craddock? I think I have heard *about* him but can't say that I ever heard *him*!" To read through the stories in this book is certainly not the same experience as hearing him tell them. It is our hope, however, that by reading through them you can catch a glimpse of Fred Craddock. We have attempted to capture elements of the oral style in which Fred speaks. Read the stories out loud and listen to the rhythms of "ordinary" speech that have extraordinary power—to reveal and conceal, to comfort and convict, to delight and teach. For those of you who read these stories for the first time, we hope that you will find him here, pointing to places in his life where the truth of the Christian gospel broke through into the clearing. Others will be "listening" to these stories again. That is the nature of stories—they live to be told and retold in God's loop of memory and imagination.

If you were to ask a preacher friend to tell you what her favorite Craddock story is, she might recall one of the stories compiled in this book. Or she might well say, "The one where I heard him for the first time!" For some it was at a conference in a large auditorium (with Fred standing on a box behind the pulpit!), for others it was in the sanctuary of a rural church; still others heard him for the first time in the chapel service at the seminary. Any one of Fred's listeners could tell you the way that he first "hooked" them into hearing—with a quip off the cuff, a self-deprecating joke, or the treble music of his voice. Or they might even tell you about the way he wrestled with a troublesome biblical text right before their eyes until it gave up its blessing. Sooner or later the talk will come around to the stories themselves. It is hard to think of Fred's preaching without recalling how stories punctuate his sermons. Some come from literature, many from the scriptures, but most from the canon of his life.

Whether Fred is stepping into the pulpit, behind the table, or onto the dais in front of the classroom, he becomes a storyteller. The arts of teaching, preaching, and storytelling enjoy a long, enduring marriage in Fred's ministry of proclamation.

Fred will nod when you use the adjective *inductive* to describe his preaching. He will certainly pause before answering the question: *Are you a "narrative" preacher?* That may surprise you at first. So many narrative or storytelling preachers claim Fred as a primary influence on their own development as preachers. Stories show up in Fred's sermons like the surprise appearance of old friends. However, narrative covers so much acreage in the field that it's hard to put a fence around it. You can easily get into a debate about what narrative preaching is and what it isn't and whether Fred is an example or not. Why bother with that? The point is that narrative has earned its place in the preacher's glossary because it has helped some of us find our way into the pulpit, some who might never have gotten there by any other way. It is also a way that we have been taught to think about our listeners. Storytelling is the way that all people give order and meaning to their experience.

In this book we have a particular set of stories that come from Fred's world. They are stories that have (as Fred himself might say) some "sweat on them"—the kind of sweat that breaks out on the back of a Tennessee farmer, the sides of the chalice at the table or the water bucket drawn from the well, the neck of the preacher in the Disciples' church, or the brow of the graduate student in the Vanderbilt library. We never tire of hearing them because they taste like salt—the kind of saltiness that Jesus talks about. You could describe the people that populate these stories as "the salt of the earth." They become so real to us in Fred's stories that they guide us across the threshold of grace. The lingering affect of Fred's own narrative material—his personal stories and recollections, the parables he lifts from scripture and everyday life, and his trunk full of literary images—has helped tune our ears to our own stories and train our eyes inward to see ourselves. The word that has the most resonance in the swirling world of stories we live in is the word that is formed on our lips and shaped in our hearts.

If you were to ask us what our favorite Craddock story is, we would tell you: "The one where we visited him at his home in Blue Ridge, Georgia," which is another story altogether.

Fred Craddock's Story

If you drive about two hours to the north of Atlanta on Highway 5, you come to a town called Cherry Log, Georgia. That's where Fred Craddock lives. The farther out of Atlanta you go, the more rolling and lush the hills become, eventually giving way to the Blue Ridge Mountains, the southernmost part of the Appalachians. Everywhere you look in this part of the state are hills covered with pines. Cherry Log is situated on Highway 5 between Elijay to the south and Blue Ridge farther up the road. Blue Ridge is where Fred gets his mail and where folks come from miles around to look for bargains in the antique stores.

Not so in Cherry Log! In Cherry Log there is The Pink Pig, a barbecue restaurant off to the right, where sauce-smothered pork is piled high on your plate. In Cherry Log there is also a church, Cherry Log Christian Church (Disciples of Christ). It's not really on the highway. The short road off to the left winds up a steep hill, and nestled among the pines is the relatively new building, with an even newer addition. Every Sunday morning at 9:45 Fred teaches the forty or so folks who show up for Bible study. An hour later they stand to stretch and welcome those arriving for worship at eleven o'clock, usually about one hundred thirty folks in all.

On a hot weekend in July the two of us have come to visit with Fred and Nettie. We arrive on Saturday afternoon and go out to dinner that evening. Over the smells of pan-fried fish, country ham, fresh vegetables, homemade bread with apple butter, and sweet tea, we tell stories. And the stories come. And so do the desserts—freshly baked pies and cakes.

Afterward, we follow Fred and Nettie back to their home. The paved road off the highway gives way to gravel. Soon two lanes give way to one. We turn into the driveway and gasp. It is not so much the house, a lovely home of gray cedar, beautiful in its own right. No, it is the land and the house—and the water. It is all of them together! A river runs through it, well, not exactly, but close. The stone-banked creek cascades down the hill on the back side of their property and goes right under their home, a kind of bridge straddling the creek. It is gorgeous. Out back are several decks, some on one side of the creek, some on the other.

It is Nettie who tells us the story of the land, about the old mill that used to be here. She shows us the stones from the mill that are still standing, witnesses to an era gone by. The sun is fading into the hillside, and on the deck we tell stories well into the Georgia darkness. "I recall one time," Fred begins, "when I was lecturing at a seminary and during a time of fellowship with the faculty, one of them blurted out, 'Fred, tell us a story!'

Not a certain story. Not a story appropriate to the moment. Not a story brought to mind. Just tell us a story!" Fred pauses, then says, "That fellow didn't understand a thing about stories or storytelling." We listen for hours to Fred's stories, and we realize that we have entered not only personal ground but holy ground really, one preacher's encounters with God.

The bugs chase us inside eventually, and the Craddocks chase us out even later. Back at the motel in Blue Ridge, we marvel at the life and ministry of Fred B. Craddock that have brought us all together this weekend. It is a long way from Kansas City and Denver, where we teach, to Cherry Log, Georgia. In some respects, it is an even longer journey from Humboldt, Tennessee, where Fred was born in 1928.

Brenning Craddock, as he was called then, spent his early years on a farm where his dad raised fruits and vegetables. His mother stuck Buster Brown stickers in the heels of shoes at the Brown Shoe Company. It was his mother who had given him to God when he was an infant. He had such a bad case of the whooping cough that she gave him up for dead at one point and went out to the barn so she would not have to listen to him gasping for air. In the barn that day she offered him to God. He recovered, but would not find out about this until years later.

The Craddock family lost the farm and eventually moved into town when Brenning was about eight or nine years old. He still recalls how devastating this was to his parents. Times were so hard that they actually had to borrow coal ash from neighbors to start a fire of their own. He and his siblings helped make ends meet by selling papers and mowing the lawn of the nearby cemetery. As might be expected, good country people also gave them things. These are the kinds of deeds that would come to inform the rural stories of Fred's preaching.

It was after the Craddocks had moved into town that some ladies from the Central Avenue Christian Church reached out to the family. They brought some shoes that fit little Brenning and a picture book with stories from the Bible. As a result of both gifts, he started going to Sunday school in the Christian church. His mother had grown up going to church, with what he fondly calls "an *In His Steps* kind of Christianity." Fred's mother encouraged him in spiritual matters, while his father, a gifted storyteller, instilled in him a love for stories. As a young man, Fred watched as many of his friends in church made commitments to vocational ministry, but not Fred. For one thing, he did not want to take such a matter lightly. For another thing, the size of pulpits and the voices of those who filled them were overwhelming to him. Even when he did entertain the idea of becoming a minister, his school counselor and his pastor advised against it.

During Fred's senior year of high school something pivotal happened. At church camp there was a night of consecration down by the lake. Afterward, the counselor encouraged the youth to return to their bunks in silence and write a letter to themselves about what they were experiencing. The letters were to be mailed out the next January. Fred remembers receiving the letter and saying yes to ministry. His mother was pleased, and that is when she told him about her dedicating him to the Lord when he was sick as a child.

After high school, Fred went to Johnson Bible College, a conservative school that required intensive study in the biblical languages, both of which he still reads well, though he admits his Greek is better than his Hebrew. At Johnson, he was required to memorize the content of each chapter of the New Testament and to memorize large portions of the New Testament in Greek. While attending Johnson, he served as pastor in two small churches that he reached by Greyhound bus every weekend, Glen Alice Christian Church and Post Oak Christian Church.

In college, however, he was not given much encouragement toward a ministry of preaching. After his first speech in class, the teacher blurted out, "Do it again. I didn't hear a word you said." Fred was so determined to strengthen his voice that he would go out to a nearby pasture regularly and preach to the cows. He thought if he could get Holsteins to raise their heads, he would be heard in the churches.

He met and fell in love with Nettie Dungan. They were married in June after graduating from Johnson. Fifty years later they are still in love, with her name mentioned in many a "Craddock story." They spent the summer of 1950 preaching at various churches, always traveling by bus because they did not have a car. When it came time to go to seminary, they visited Christian Theological Seminary in Indianapolis and Vanderbilt Divinity School in Nashville, but the Graduate Seminary of Phillips University seemed like home, being located in rural Enid, Oklahoma. Fred started there in the fall of 1950, finishing in 1953.

In his seminary preaching classes, he was schooled in the traditional approach of John Broadus' monumental work *On the Preparation and Delivery of Sermons*. All those sermons, regardless of the text and occasion, sounded the same. It was the kind of preaching Fred heard growing up. G. Edwin Osborn was his professor, a man who had once been a dispatcher for trains, a job in which everything was highly structured. That was how Fred was taught to preach—Roman numerals, capital A and B, little ones and twos.

It was at Phillips that faculty members encouraged him to think of becoming a teacher some day. Over time the idea grew on him, so after graduating and serving a church in Custer City, Oklahoma, Fred went back to Johnson Bible College, where he taught from 1953 to 1957, seeing one class all the way through.

While serving as pastor in Columbia, Tennessee, he began his doctoral studies at Vanderbilt and began to experiment with storytelling as a way of preaching. The members of the church commented more than once on how his informal talks at church socials were so natural and interesting. "For instance," he recalls, "in the fellowship hall after a meal, I found myself using scripture and people's experiences, telling anecdotes from my life, and bringing it home to the point of the occasion. But then in the sanctuary on Sunday morning, I'd manufacture something else that I thought a sermon must be."

Fred was hesitant to try storytelling approaches to preaching for several reasons, one being his weak voice. His effort to be heard meant there was no room for modulation, the kind of thing required in storytelling. In addition, his mother frequently used the word *story* as a synonym for lying. She even made it into a verb. "Don't story me," she used to say. She did not consider stories to be appropriate in sermons. Yet Fred's father had instilled in him a love for literature, especially Shakespeare. Slowly, he began to experiment with storytelling in the less-formal Sunday evening services in Columbia.

After finishing his doctoral course work in 1961, he went on to teach at Phillips at the undergraduate level while he completed his dissertation. Five years later, he began to teach in the seminary at Phillips. It was there that he was asked to teach a course titled "From Text to Sermon." The intent was to show the practicalities of exegesis. He still recalls being fascinated with what he describes as "the sermon being the future of the text." One of his great contributions to preaching theory has been a sharing of his own instinctive genius, bringing to the conscious level what he did naturally on his own when preparing a sermon. It was not easy to do at first, he notes, "It was like watching your feet while you walked."

His publishing *As One Without Authority* was not intended to revolutionize preaching theory, a discipline not held in high esteem at the time. He simply wanted to help his students preach with integrity. The title itself was originally intended as a humble reflection that this was not his field. He later found the phrase in the writings of Søren Kierkegaard, who would become a key figure in Fred's work.

During the academic year of 1968–69, he was on sabbatical leave in Germany. A couple of the chapters for his book were already written, but he felt that German scholarship might be able to help him think through some issues yet unclear in his mind. In particular, he had gone to study with Hermann Diem who, as it turns out, had been forced into early retirement because of alcoholism. On a narrow street in Tübingen, between the university and the Neckar River, Diem told Fred that he was wasting his time, to go back home. Then, in passing, he blurted out the name of Kierkegaard. "Study Kierkegaard," Diem told him. It was a providential moment. The writings of Kierkegaard helped Craddock to finish *As One Without Authority* and became the major force behind his 1978 Lyman Beecher Lectures at Yale, which were published under the title *Overhearing the Gospel.*

From 1979 to 1993, Craddock served as Bandy Distinguished Professor of Preaching and New Testament at Candler School of Theology, Emory University, in Atlanta, Georgia. While there, his reputation grew through lectureships and numerous publications in New Testament studies and homiletics, including his introductory textbook in homiletics, *Preaching.*

Upon retiring from Candler, Fred had planned to conduct workshops in preaching for uneducated ministers in the rural Appalachians. He had not planned on becoming the preaching minister at Cherry Log Christian Church. That happened while doing some supply preaching at a church in Blue Ridge, near where he and his wife had retired. It was the people in the community who encouraged him to help them start a church.

Although Fred preaches at Cherry Log almost every week, a search committee has been formed to call a pastor. When a pastor is finally called, Fred will help in whatever way he can, but hopes to give himself more fully to workshops for rural pastors. In the meantime, he is the Cherry Log congregation's pastor. In his study, he can close his eyes and see the folks who worship there on Sundays.

On this particular Sunday morning in July, we drive down the highway to Cherry Log knowing that today's Sunday school lesson is on the parables of Jesus. How appropriate, since in many ways, Fred's stories are parables, what C. H. Dodd described as the kinds of stories that leave listeners in doubt about precise meanings and that tease folks into wrestling with what they mean. Not surprisingly, that is what Fred does in Bible study this morning.

In the worship service, the congregation celebrates the music ministry of the church, dedicating new choir robes and recognizing the gifts of those who lead in worship. There is no sermon per se, not today. Instead, Fred shares a communion meditation as we gather at the Lord's table.

After Sunday school and morning worship, we gather at another table. We go to The Pink Pig for lunch, where the smells are scrumptious and the surroundings are unimpressive, except for the picture of Jimmy and Rosalynn Carter hanging on the wall. Fred introduces us to the owner, who is busy cooking. Over lunch we tell more stories and talk "preaching." We wonder if Fred realizes that his favorite expression for starting a story is "I recall." We wonder if he realizes what powerful effects his stories have had on people over the years. We wonder if he realizes how many preachers on any given Sunday tell a "Craddock story."

Later that evening we gather again at Fred and Nettie's home. We talk about this collection of stories taking shape. It was our idea all along, not Fred's. He honestly wonders why anyone would want to read his stories. Still, if it's going to happen, there are some things concerning the book about which he feels strongly. He insists, for instance, that there be no index—not a topical one ("They're parables," he says), not even an index of key words ("Preaching is hard work. Let them hunt for it!"). He insists that the stories be told in his own words, not ours or anybody else's. He hopes that readers will treat the stories with respect. Fred also wonders how the stories will be arranged. "How do you fellows plan to organize the collection?" he asks.

That is a good question, one that demands a really good answer, or at least a story, a parable of sorts. During the worship service earlier that morning, Fred did not preach. Not exactly. Instead, he shared a meditation at the time of communion. He began by asking, "How far back can you remember?" He noted that he's heard of people who claim to remember way back into their childhood, as early as when they were two or three years old. He said that on a clear day he can sometimes remember clear back to creation, God's creating the world with a word. On a clear day he can sometimes remember back to the cross on which Jesus died and that glorious day in which he was raised from the dead. "How far back can you remember?" he asked the congregation.

Later, in the motel room, we marvel. Oh sure, we had hoped to hear a sermon, but we marvel at Fred's simple yet powerful meditation. We wonder if most folks remember the first Craddock story they ever heard. We wonder aloud if we remember the first time we heard Fred tell a story. We ask about each other's favorite Craddock stories. Then we recall how the idea for this collection came about in the first place.

In November 1992, the two of us were in Kansas City for a workshop on biblical storytelling. At lunch that day some of the ministers who were gathered around one of the tables spontaneously began to share their favorite Craddock stories. Well, almost; they would begin with the phrase, "My favorite is the one about…," but that was nearly the end of each telling. No one actually told a complete story. We simply referred to one, and everyone nodded. "My favorite is the one about jury duty." "That's a good one, but what about the barbecue restaurant?" "Oh yeah, that's good, but what about…?" We knew then and there that some day these stories, these Craddock stories, would have to be collected.

We decided on only one rule. All the stories in this book come straight from Fred Craddock's mouth. We found them on audiotape, on videotape, or in print, or we heard them directly from Fred. We've tried to preserve his own wording. Although there are many other stories that we—and many other people—remember hearing Fred tell, these are the ones where we knew Fred's own words to tell the story. If you know more, feel free to send them to us—or at least tell them to one another.

Back in the motel, we wrestle with Fred's question about arranging all these stories. Maybe alphabetical based on the first line, like so many collections of poetry. No, that won't work. People know Fred's stories by the punch line, not the first line. Maybe they could be arranged purely at random, no rhyme or reason whatsoever. Definitely not! We wonder how Fred would arrange them. We wonder if he has his own favorites, and if so, what those might be. Later that day we ask, "Fred, do you have a favorite or two?" He smiles. "Of course!" he says. "Of course!"

Mike Graves
Richard F. Ward

Stories from
Fred Craddock

My mother took us to church and Sunday school; my father didn't go. He complained about Sunday dinner being late when she came home. Sometimes the preacher would call, and my father would say, "I know what the church wants. Church doesn't care about me. Church wants another name, another pledge, another name, another pledge. Right? Isn't that the name of it? Another name, another pledge." That's what he always said.

Sometimes we'd have a revival. Pastor would bring the evangelist and say to the evangelist, "There's one now, sic him, get him, get him," and my father would say the same thing. Every time, my mother in the kitchen, always nervous, in fear of flaring tempers, of somebody being hurt. And always my father said, "The church doesn't care about me. The church wants another name and another pledge." I guess I heard it a thousand times.

One time he didn't say it. He was in the veteran's hospital, and he was down to seventy-three pounds. They'd taken out his throat, and said, "It's too late." They put in a metal tube, and X rays burned him to pieces. I flew in to see him. He couldn't speak, couldn't eat. I looked around the room, potted plants and cut flowers on all the windowsills, a stack of cards twenty inches deep beside his bed. And even that tray where they put food, if you can eat, on that was a flower. And all the flowers beside the bed, every card, every blossom, were from persons or groups from the church.

He saw me read a card. He could not speak, so he took a Kleenex box and wrote on the side of it a line from Shakespeare. If he had not written this line, I would not tell you this story. He wrote: "In this harsh world, draw your breath in pain to tell my story."

I said, "What is your story, Daddy?"

And he wrote, "I was wrong."

Boredom is a preview of death, if not itself a form of death, and when trapped in prolonged boredom, even the most saintly of us will hope for, pray for, or even engineer relief, however demonic. Sincere Sunday worshipers will confess to welcoming in muffled celebration any interruption of the funeral droning. Be honest: Have you ever quietly cheered when a child fell off a pew, a bird flew in a window, the lights went out, the organ wheezed, the sound system picked up police calls, or a dog came down the aisle and curled up to sleep below the pulpit? Passengers on cruise ships, after nine beautiful sunsets and eighty-six invigorating games of shuffleboard, begin to ask the crew hopefully, "Do you think we'll have a storm?"

I recently heard a quiet and passive clergyman tell of his attending the Indianapolis 500. He confessed that after two hours of watching the same cars speed by again and again, the boredom turned him into a degenerate sinner. At first, he said, he simply entertained thoughts of "What if…?"; and his own imagination thrilled him. But soon his boredom demanded more. A car caught on fire. Hurrah! Not until later did he remind himself that he, a Christian minister, had experienced no concern for the driver. But a burning car was not enough; something more dramatic was needed to effect a resurrection from the death of boredom. Voices within him, he admitted, began to call for a smash-up. The demon of boredom had totally transformed him. Shift the scene to a classroom or sanctuary, subject him or you or me to repeated and prolonged boredom, and a similar process begins. For the communicating of the Christian faith, formally or informally, to be boring is not simply "too bad," to be glossed over with the usual "But he is really a genuine fellow," or "But she is very sincere." Boredom works against the faith by provoking contrary thoughts or lulling us to sleep or draping the whole occasion with a pall of indifference and unimportance.

As a boy I spent pleasant summer evenings gathering fallen stars. As I think back on it, the spent stars were worthless, but it was something to do. My brothers and I would go into a field near the house, climb up on tree stumps (all that remained after the blight of a once-beautiful chestnut grove), and wait for stars to fall. From these perches we could see exactly where they fell, and it was not uncommon to have our pockets filled within an hour. Sometimes, whether in greed or out of compassion for fallen stars that might otherwise go unnoticed, we would sneak from the back porch with Grandma's clothes basket and harvest the remaining stars still flickering on the ground. And sometimes, dragging the heavy basket home left us too tired to empty it. "We will do it in the morning," we would say, but in the morning Grandma was already fussing about a residue of gray ashes in her clothes basket. (Everyone knows you cannot save stars over until the next night.) We denied charges of having kindled a fire in her basket and snickered off to play, protected from punishment by the mystery.

But during her last illness, Grandma called me to her bed and told me, almost secretively, that she knew what we had been doing with her basket. My guilty silence was broken by her instruction for me to bring to her a package wrapped in newspaper from the bottom of an old chest. I obeyed and then waited the eternity it took for her arthritic fingers to open the bundle. "Oh, it's gone," she said, showing me where it had been. In the bottom of the package was a little residue of gray ashes. We stared at each other.

"You too, Grandma? Why didn't you tell me?"

"I was afraid you would laugh at me. And why didn't you tell me?"

"I was afraid you would scold me."

In a certain village the school bell rang at 8:30 a.m. to call the children to class. The boys and girls left their homes and toys reluctantly, creeping like snails into the school, not late but not a second early. The bell rang again at 3:30 p.m., releasing the children to homes and toys, to which they rushed at the very moment of the tolling of the bell. This is how it was every day, with every child except one. She came early to help the teacher prepare the room and materials for the day. She stayed late to help the teacher clean the board, dust erasers, and put away materials. And during the day she sat close to the teacher, all eyes and ears for the lessons being taught. One day when noise and inattention were worse than usual, the teacher called the class to order. Pointing to the little girl in the front row, the teacher said, "Why can you not be as she is? She comes early to help, she stays late to help, and all day long she is attentive and courteous."

"It isn't fair to ask us to be as she is," said one boy from the rear of the room.

"Why?"

"Because she has an advantage," he replied.

"I don't understand. What is her advantage?" asked the puzzled teacher.

"She is an orphan," he almost whispered as he sat down.

There once was an old man whose only close friend was his dog. The love between them had deepened through the years. Now both had begun to feel the pain and burden of age. The dog, twelve years old, could hardly walk and was covered with an irritating rash. The old man lifted the dog into his arms and carried it to the car where it lay on the seat beside him on the way to see the veterinarian. From the parking lot the old man carried the dog gently inside. "Can I help you?" asked the veterinarian.

The old man, still holding his dog, said, "First, I must ask you a question. Do you love animals above everything else?"

"Well, I love God first. Jesus says in Mark 12:30, 'You shall love the Lord your God with all your heart, and with all your soul, and with all your mind, and with all your strength.' And of course a second command is to love thy neighbor as oneself. We must put these things first, and then we can think about the animals."

"Then I must go elsewhere," said the old man as he moved toward the door.

"Why? What is wrong?"

"This dog is my friend," explained the old man, "and I feel I can trust him only to the care of a veterinarian who is a Christian."

I recall some years ago taking over a class for an ailing colleague. It was an Old Testament class, but he had the good grace to become ill far enough in advance to allow me to prepare. One hates to be a total fool, even when out of one's field. A night and a day I spent in the deep of the assignment, Psalm 91. Hebrew language, poetry, history, liturgy, and commentary were waded through in order to reach the podium. The students, having heard they were to endure a substitute, outstripped their own excellent record of nonpreparation. Outwardly, of course, I growled, but privately I welcomed ignorance not only as unthreatening but as granting full release to my own recent wisdom. Against the dark backgrounds of their empty minds I cast the clear diamonds of critical analysis. For two hours the text was subjected to the best methods of biblical criticism.

At the conclusion of the seminar we joined the entire seminary in the chapel to hold a memorial service for a respected teacher who had died suddenly of a heart attack. The worship leader read the text: Psalm 91. The appropriateness of the text was apparent: The text interpreted the occasion, and the occasion interpreted the text. Afterward, some of the students who had been in the seminar, in a mood of anti-academia, spoke to me in praise of the chapel service and in criticism of the apparent uselessness and sterility of our classroom exercise. In no way, they said, did our analysis of Psalm 91 compare with the immediacy and clarity of the reading in worship. There was truth to what they said; there is light upon the page in the sanctuary that seldom comes in the classroom. Nevertheless, I reminded the students that we did not just hum the psalm in the chapel; we had attended to words, to a message from the psalmist for a particular occasion. We talked in the hallway at length about what that message was and listened to comments by students who were in the chapel but not in the seminar. Before long two observations were made: First, while all in the chapel were moved by the appropriateness of the text, probably none present quite grasped the meaning and power of Psalm 91 as did those who had carefully studied it; and second, classroom and sanctuary should and do serve each other in the service of God.

There was a certain man who moved into a cottage equipped with a stove and simple furnishings. As the sharp edge of winter cut across the landscape, the cottage grew cold, as did its occupant. He went out back and pulled a few boards off the house to kindle a fire. The fire was warm, but the house seemed as cold as before. More boards came off for a larger fire to warm the now even colder house, which in turn required an even larger fire, demanding more boards. In a few days the man cursed the weather, cursed the house, cursed the stove, and moved away.

I recall in a class on the parables a few years ago, the students gravitated heavily toward the stories of a reversal type in which the offer of grace was extended to the wayward son, the publican, the eleventh-hour worker, and the servant who took big risks with the master's money. These students frowned on punishing lazy stewards or slamming doors in the faces of poor girls who forgot to bring oil. In short, grace was no longer unexpected, but instead was expected by these seminarians and hence was no longer grace, and if it was, it was cheap. So I read this story once without explanation and asked if it was a parable:

There was a certain seminary professor who was very strict about due dates for papers. Due dates were announced at the beginning of a semester, and failure to meet them resulted in an F for the semester. In one class three students did not meet the deadline. The first one explained, "Professor, unexpected guests from out of state came the evening before the paper was due, and I was unable to finish it."

"Then you receive an F," said the professor.

The second student explained, "On the day before the paper was due, I became ill with influenza and was unable to complete it."

"Then you receive an F," said the professor.

The third student, visibly shaken at the news about the fate of the other two, cautiously approached the professor's desk. Slowly he began, "Professor, our first baby was due the same day the paper was due. The evening before, my wife began having pains, and so I rushed her to the hospital. Shortly after midnight she gave birth to a boy. Our son weighs eight pounds. We named him Kenneth."

The professor listened with interest, moved his chair back from the desk, and looked up at the ceiling. After a long pause, he looked across at the student and said, "Then you receive an F for the course." The news spread rapidly through the seminary. A large delegation of students came to the professor to protest.

"Why have you been so cruel and harsh?" they asked.

The professor replied, "At the beginning of the semester I gave my word concerning the papers. If the word of a teacher in a Christian seminary cannot be trusted, whose word can be trusted?" The students were dismissed.

Most of the students were angry not only with the professor in the story but with me for telling it. They insisted it was not a parable.

The impact of the biblical narrative in the Christian community is a testimony to the fact that a "Once upon a time" can be heard as a "Once for all." To abandon that narrative out of sincere desire to effect a "Once for all" experience is to have surrendered the arsenal and gone into battle with nothing more than good eye contact.

Perhaps I caricature a bit, but I remember a few years ago sitting beside a man from West Germany overhearing a Jew from England tell the story of a Jewish community in Poland. When the story ended, the German and I turned to each other, paused in silence, and moved out separately. Both of us had been addressed, confronted, encountered, called into question, and immensely assured in our hope. Distance? Yes, long ago and far away, about Jews in Poland. Participation? Yes, we were there.

There was a certain disciple who enrolled in a course offered by a rabbi. The disciple sat before the rabbi with a sheet of paper on which was written only his name. The rabbi began to speak, and the disciple took notes. In addition, the disciple read many books and, as he had been taught, took many notes. It came to pass, however, that as the course progressed the disciple discovered that the increase of his notes did not bring an increase in understanding. He stopped taking notes. In fact, he began to throw away the notes he had. On the last day of class he sat before the rabbi with a sheet of paper on which was written only his name. The disciple complained, "I have nothing to show for my investment of time and money."

The rabbi replied, "Do you not understand? This course is a parable."

I want to pause here to tell you about Rachel, but I am very hesitant. She is so quiet, and her life has been so hidden from public view that such exposure as this brief story will bring might embarrass her. Rachel recently entered a retirement home where others can be to her the family she never had. After graduation, she took a teaching job in the grade school of a small town, and there she remained for forty years, introducing children to books and ideas and to each other. Before her retirement she had taught boys and girls, and their boys and girls, and their boys and girls. Of course, she threatened to retire many weary springs, but threats by Rachel were very much like little boys' threats to run away from home. The fact is, she was pained by springtime and the simple rituals of promotion by which her boys and girls were lost to her. She felt delightfully guilty when a favorite pupil (and weren't they all favorite to her?) was detained another year. Summers and weekends were spent gathering objects to help her teaching. I wonder how many pumpkins, flags, witches, turkeys, Santa Clauses, and valentines she had stuck on her classroom windows.

No one could have been more shocked than Rachel when the chairman of the school board told her that she was being given early retirement. Do not misunderstand: She never for a moment took it as a personal criticism or lack of confidence in her abilities as a teacher. Her response was shock simply because it vibrated against her finally achieving the one ambition of her life: to become a child. Not childish, that sad state of those who try to negotiate adult life with a child's reasons and behaviors. No, I mean she became a child. Rachel moved totally out of the adult world into that of the children. Their laughter, fears, anticipations, games, pains, and friendships were hers. At Halloween, at Christmas, on Valentine's Day, she was totally a child. Finally she had done it! No more generation gap, no more distance in vocabulary and perspective and vested interest, now full rapport and perfect communication. "Poor Rachel," said the adults who had once been her pupils but had so completely moved out of a child's world that they did not recognize in her present manner the full flowering of those childlike qualities she possessed only in part when they were in her class. But finally after forty years, for the sake of the children, she had become one of them. The perfect teacher! "She will have to be retired," muttered the school board. "For the sake of the children we will have to let her go."

No parents raised an outcry; they accepted in silence the decision as painfully right. Only a newcomer, with more reason than feeling, asked why. "Because she has become like the children."

And He became in every way as we are. Of course, we had to get rid of Him.

For a brief time, I was acting dean at Phillips Seminary. It was for fifteen months. That's similar to fifteen years. The secretary said, "There's someone here to see you." A woman asked me to come out to the parking lot. I was a little nervous, but I followed her to the parking lot and to her car. She opened the back door, and slumped in the back seat was her brother. He had been a senior at the University of Oklahoma. He had been in a bad car wreck and in a coma eight months. She had quit her job as a schoolteacher to take care of him. All of their resources were gone. She opened the door and said, "I'd like for you to heal him."

I said, "I can pray for him. And I can pray with you. But I do not have the gift of healing."

She got behind the wheel and said to me, "Then what in the world do you do?" And she drove off.

What I did that afternoon was study, stare at my books, and try to forget what she had said.

If you don't have reverence for God, if you talk glibly and casually about God, how can you pray? Hallowed, sacred, holy, sanctified, is the name of God. No wonder they couldn't pronounce the name of God in Judaism in the first century. That name is hard to say.

When I was a child, my mother would play word games with us in the evening by the fire. She taught us phonic spelling. If you can say it, you can spell it. And she led us into the deep waters of *oviparous, ovoviviparous,* and *hypotenuse*. I once knew how to pronounce and spell *asafetida*. But one word she never put on the list because she knew we were just children. She never put on the list *God*.

A few years ago when I was on the West Coast to speak at a seminary, just before the first lecture, one of the students stood up and said, "Before you speak, I need to know if you are Pentecostal."

The room grew silent. I didn't know where the dean was! The student quizzed me in front of everybody.

I was taken aback, and so I said, "Do you mean if I belong to the Pentecostal church?"

He said, "No, I mean are you Pentecostal?"

I said, "Are you asking if I am charismatic?"

He said, "I am asking if you are Pentecostal."

I said, "Do you want to know if I speak in tongues?"

He said, "I want to know if you are Pentecostal."

I said, "I don't know what your question is."

He said, "Obviously, you are not Pentecostal." He left.

What are we talking about? In spite of the fact that the church doesn't know what the adjective means, the church insists that the word remain in our vocabulary as an adjective. The church is unwilling for the word simply to be a noun, to represent a date, a place, or an event in the history of the church; it refuses for it to be simply a memory, an item, something back there somewhere. The church insists the word is an adjective; it describes our church. The word, then, is *Pentecostal*.

G lenn Adsit, a schoolmate from years ago, ministered mostly in China. He was under house arrest in China when the soldiers came one day and said, "You can return to America."

They were celebrating, and the soldiers said, "You can take two hundred pounds with you."

Well, they'd been there for years. Two hundred pounds. They got the scales and started the family arguments: two children, wife, husband. Must have this vase. Well, this is a new typewriter. What about my books? What about this? And they weighed everything and took it off and weighed this and took it off and weighed this and, finally, right on the dot, two hundred pounds.

The soldier asked, "Ready to go?"

"Yes."

"Did you weigh everything?"

"Yes."

"You weighed the kids?"

"No, we didn't."

"Weigh the kids."

And in a moment, typewriter and vase and all became trash. Trash. It happens.

When I was pastoring in Tennessee, there was a girl about seven years old who came to our church regularly for Sunday school, and sometimes her parents let her stay for the worship service. They didn't come. We had a circular drive at that church. It was built for people who let their children off and drove on. We didn't want to inconvenience them, so we had a circular drive. But they were very faithful, Mom and Dad. They had moved from New Jersey with the new chemical plant. He was upwardly mobile; they were both very ambitious; and they didn't come to church. There wasn't really any need for that, I guess.

But on Saturday nights, the whole town knew of their parties. They gave parties, not for entertainment, but as part of the upwardly mobile thing. That determined who was invited: the right people, the one just above, and finally on up to the boss. And those parties were full of drinking and wild and vulgar things. Everybody knew. But there was their beautiful girl every Sunday.

One Sunday morning I looked out, and she was there. I thought, "Well, she's with her friends," but it was her Mom and Dad. After the sermon, at the close of the service, as is the custom at my church, came an invitation to discipleship, and Mr. and Mrs. Mom and Dad came to the front. They confessed faith in Christ. Afterward I asked, "What prompted this?"

They said, "Well, do you know about our parties?"

And I said, "Yeah, I have heard about your parties."

They said, "Well, we had one last night again, and it got a little loud, it got a little rough, and there was too much drinking. We waked our daughter, and she came downstairs to about the third step. She saw that we were eating and drinking, and she said, 'Oh, can I say the blessing? God is great, God is good, let us thank him for our food. Good-night, everybody.' She went back upstairs. 'Oh, my land, it's time to go, we've got to be going.' 'We've stayed way too long.' Within two minutes the room was empty.'"

Mr. and Mrs. Mom and Dad began cleaning up, picking up crumpled napkins and wasted and spilled peanuts and half sandwiches, and taking empty glasses on trays to the kitchen. And with two trays, he and she met on either side of the sink, they looked at each other, and he expressed what both were thinking: "Where do we think we're going?" The moment of truth.

The Bible calls it a new birth. You've been to that window, haven't you—the maternity ward, the nursery, and all that stuff up there in that big window? With all the men outside trying to figure out which one is theirs? You know, "Julie is in there somewhere, and I know she's the prettiest one." You can't read those little old bands, where the arm comes down and the hand joins and there's a deep wrinkle, and there's that band. It's so small, and you say, "Well, I think that's her???!!!" And the Bible says, That's what it is; that is it.

A family is out for a drive on a Sunday afternoon. It is a pleasant afternoon, and they relax at a leisurely pace down the highway. Suddenly, the two children begin to beat their father in the back: "Daddy, Daddy, stop the car! There's a kitten back there on the side of the road!"

The father says, "So there's a kitten on the side of the road. We're having a drive."

"But Daddy, you must stop and pick it up."

"I don't have to stop and pick it up."

"But Daddy, if you don't, it will die."

"Well then, it will have to die. We don't have room for another animal. We have a zoo already at the house. No more animals."

"But Daddy, are you going to just let it die?"

"Be quiet, children; we're trying to have a pleasant drive."

"We never thought our Daddy would be so mean and cruel as to let a kitten die."

Finally the mother turns to her husband and says, "Dear, you'll have to stop." He turns the car around, returns to the spot, and pulls off to the side of the road. "You kids stay in the car. I'll see about it." He goes out to pick up the little kitten, who is just skin and bones, sore-eyed, and full of fleas. When he reaches down to pick it up, with its last bit of energy the kitten bristles, baring tooth and claw. Hisss! He picks up the kitten by the loose skin at the neck, brings it over to the car, and says, "Don't touch it. It's probably got leprosy."

Back home they go. When they get to the house the children give the kitten several baths, about a gallon of warm milk, and intercede: "Can we let it stay in the house just tonight? Tomorrow we'll fix it a place in the garage."

The father says, "Sure, take my bedroom; the whole house is already a zoo." They fix a comfortable bed, fit for a pharaoh. Several weeks pass. Then one day the father walks in, feels something rub against his leg, looks down, and there is a cat. He reaches down toward the cat, carefully checking to see that no one is watching. When the cat sees his hand, it does not bare its claws and hiss; instead it arches its back to receive a caress. Is that the same cat? It couldn't be the same cat. It's not the same as that frightened, hurt, hissing kitten on the side of the road. Of course not, and you know as well as I what makes the difference.

Not too long ago God reached out a hand to bless me and my family. When God did, I looked at that hand; it was covered with scratches. Such is the hand of love, extended to those who are bitter.

I am going to say a word. The moment I say the word I want you to see a face, to recall a face and a name, someone who comes to your mind when I say the word. Are you ready? The word is *bitter.* Bitter. Do you see a face? I see a face. I see the face of a farmer in western Oklahoma, riding a mortgaged tractor, burning gasoline purchased on credit, moving across rented land, rearranging the dust. Bitter.

Do you see a face? I see the face of a woman forty-seven years old. She sits out on a hillside, drawn and confused under a green canopy furnished by the mortuary. She is banked on all sides by flowers sprinkled with cards: "You have our condolences." Bitter.

Do you see a face? I see the face of a man who runs a small grocery store. His father ran the store in that neighborhood for twenty years, and he is now in his twelfth year there. The grocery doesn't make much profit, but it keeps the family together. It's a business. There are no customers in the store now, and the grocer stands in the doorway with his apron rolled up around his waist, looking across the street where workmen are completing a supermarket. Bitter.

I see the face of a young couple. They seem to be about nineteen. They are standing in the airport terminal, holding hands so tightly that their knuckles are white. She's pregnant; he's dressed in military green. They are not talking, just standing and looking at each other. The loudspeaker comes on: "Flight 392 now loading at gate 22, yellow concourse, all aboard for San Francisco." He slowly moves toward the gate; she stands there alone. Bitter.

Do you see a face? A young minister in a small town, in a cracker box of a house they call the parsonage. He lives there with his wife and small child. On Saturday morning there is a knock at the door. He answers, and there standing before him on the porch is the chairman of his church board, who is also the president of the local bank, and owner of most of the land round about. He has in his hands a small television. It is an old television, small screen, black-and-white. It's badly scarred, and one of the knobs is off. He says: "My wife and I got one of those new twenty-five-inch color sets, but they didn't want to take this one on trade, so I just said to myself, *Well, we'll just give it to the minister. That's probably the reason our ministers don't stay any longer than they do. We don't do enough nice things for them.* The young minister looks up and tries to smile and say thanks. But I want you to see his face. Bitter.

Will you look at one other face? His name is Saul. Saul of Tarsus.

It's an image problem. It is very difficult to move past that, sometimes if it's positive, sometimes if it's negative. The committee said to the young minister being interviewed, "You've preached a real good sermon; that's as good a sermon as we've had in this church in a long time. And you've answered the questions. Your theology and your biblical knowledge are really good, and your references are good, but we just don't feel like you're the one for our church just now."

And she says, "Oh."

Recently, one of our students, a woman, in tears told me that she walked into Brooks commons and saw a friend of hers sitting reading something. She said, "I was busy getting some money out of my purse to get a pop out of the machine. I just said to my friend over there, 'Well how are you doing?'"

She continued, "I found out later her response was, 'I just got a letter from my mother. She has a malignancy, and I think I'm going to have to go home to help her.'"

In tears the student said to me, "I didn't hear. I just went on and got my drink, came back out, and said, 'Well, what have you got planned for the weekend?' Did not hear a thing."

What would it be like if we really did hear everything?

I have a student who, for eight years, taught in a school in Nashville, Tennessee, for children with hearing disorders. Their ears were all right; they just didn't make contact. He said that after eight years, "I just could not stand it anymore. I went home crying; I went to work crying." He said, "One year, right after the Thanksgiving holiday, there was this beautiful girl in the school. Heather was her name. She was seven years old. We were out on the playground just after our Thanksgiving holiday. I went over to Heather, took her by the shoulders, squatted down in front of her, and said, 'Heather? Heather, what did you eat for Thanksgiving?'

"Heather said, 'My shoes are red.'"

He said to me, "I just, I just couldn't do it anymore."

I didn't have the heart to tell him that he's going to have experiences pretty close to that. I was in Dallas in a service in which the music, the anthem, the prayers, the songs, everything gelled, and in the sermon, everything was just right. I was in the presence of God. Standing there after the benediction, I didn't want to move. I was immobilized by the presence of God in the service. Just a guest. A man in the pew in front of me—he didn't know me, I didn't know him—turned around and said, "Do you think Tom Landry's going to coach the Cowboys another year?"

Do you know what the man said to me? The man said, "My shoes are red."

We had a dinner guest in our home who was spending the night. As I read the paper, he played with our kids and taught them a new game. How long had it been since I had come home from work, got down on the floor, and played with the kids and taught them a new game? I was judged by that.

Following dinner, he said to Mrs. Craddock, "I certainly appreciate the meal. That was just a wonderful meal." I tried to remember when it was that I had said that to my wife following dinner. I think it was in '49.

He went out for a walk and came back in and said, "Oh, those are nice folks next door. I met Mr. Yung and his wife from Seoul. Very nice young couple." Well, I had heard some Koreans moved in down there, but I didn't know. When he said their first names, I was judged.

Just a familiar pattern: Come home, read the paper, and eat supper. Then here comes someone strange. Everything looks different, and I think, "Where in the world have I been?"

First little church I served was in the eastern Tennessee hills, not too far from Oak Ridge. When Oak Ridge began to boom with the atomic energy, that little bitty town became a booming city just overnight. Every hill and every valley and every shady grove had recreational vehicles and trucks and things like that. People came in from everywhere and pitched tents, lived in wagons. Hard hats from everywhere, with their families and children paddling around in the mud in those trailer parks, lived in everything temporarily to work. Our church was not far away. We had a beautiful little church—white frame building, one hundred and twelve years old. The church had an organ in the corner, which one of the young fellows had to pump while Ms. Lois played it. Boy, she could play the songs just as slow as anybody.

The organ was a little slow. The church had beautifully decorated chimneys, kerosene lamps all around the walls, and every pew in this little church was hewn, hand hewn, from a giant poplar tree. After church one Sunday morning I asked the leaders to stay. I said to them, "Now we need to launch a calling campaign and an invitational campaign in all those trailer parks to invite those people to church."

"Oh, I don't know. I don't think they'd fit in here," one of them said. "They're just here temporarily, just construction people. They'll be leaving pretty soon."

"Well, we ought to invite them, make them feel at home," I said.

We argued about it, time ran out, and we said we'd vote next Sunday. Next Sunday, we all sat down after the service. "I move," said one of them, "I move that in order to be a member of this church, you must own property in the county."

Someone else said, "I second that." It passed. I voted against it, but they reminded me that I was just a kid preacher and I didn't have a vote. It passed. When we moved back to these parts, I took my wife to see that little church, because I had told her that painful, painful story. The roads have changed. The interstate goes through that part of the country, so I had a hard time finding it, but I finally did. I found the state road, the county road, and the little gravel road. Then there, back among the pines, was that building shining white. It was different. The parking lot was full—motorcycles and trucks and cars packed in there. And out front, a great big sign: *Barbecue, all you can eat.* It's a restaurant, so we went inside. The pews are against a wall. They have electric lights now, and the organ pushed over into the corner. There are all these aluminum and plastic tables, and people sitting there eating barbecued pork and chicken and ribs—all kinds of people. Parthians and Medes and Edomites and dwellers of Mesopotamia, all kinds of people. I said to Nettie, "It's a good thing this is not still a church, otherwise these people couldn't be in here."

I remember in an airport in Kansas City years ago, waiting for a plane, I fell into conversation with a fellow from the University of Utrecht in the Netherlands. He was in this country completing a monograph, a study on the influence of the conversation between doctors and nurses with the patient in surgery who is under anesthesia. His view was, in fact, that he had established it beyond all doubt. He found that if the doctors and nurses were negative and gripey and grumpy, then the patient in post-operative conditions was depressed and pessimistic. If the doctors and nurses were upbeat, happy, merry, and cheerful, then the patient in post-operative care was euphoric and optimistic and proceeded to recover quickly. The time came when I had to catch my plane. I thanked him for the conversation, and he said, "Why, are you a doctor?"

I said, "Oh, no, I'm a preacher. But if it'll work in surgery, it'll work in sanctuary." So when I go somewhere to speak, and people are asleep, it doesn't bother me, because I know that several days later they may get a little Christian twitch. They won't know what caused it, but I'll know.

It happened to me in Chicago, at Rockefeller Chapel. There was a woman there who was showing me where to go, where to stand, what not to do, and this and that. I visited with her after the sermon in a little coffee conversation, and she said, "Have we met?" I said, "No, why?" When she said, "Well, you act like you know me," I remembered her name was Mignonne. When I was a child, my Sunday school teacher who taught me the Psalms and the stories about Jesus when I was in just kindergarten, her name was Mignonne Williams, a very kind and sweet woman. I had attributed to this woman all of the grace and beauty of Mignonne.

W hen I was baptized, I was fourteen years old. I know the minister was saying a lot of wonderful things about being buried with Christ and all of that—I'm sure he was; he was a good minister. But I was just thinking, *Do I hold the handkerchief? Does he hold the handkerchief? Uh, I wonder if it's cold…and I bet it's deep too.*

I'm having all these thoughts, and the minister is saying, "You're buried with Christ, and…" It just seems that we learn things afterward; it's in reflection and in memory that we learn it.

I went to see a lady in our church who was facing surgery. I went to see her in the hospital. She had never been in the hospital before, and the surgery was major. I walked in there. She was a nervous wreck, and she started crying. She wanted me to pray with her, which I did. By her bed there was a stack of books and magazines: *True Love, Mirror, Hollywood Today,* stuff about Elizabeth Taylor and folk. She just had a stack of them there, and she was a wreck. It occurred to me, *There's not a calorie in that whole stack to help her through her experience.* She had no place to dip down into a reservoir and come up with something—a word, a phrase, a thought, an idea, a memory, a person. Just empty.

How marvelous is the life of the person who, like a wise homemaker, when the berries and fruits and vegetables are ripe, puts them away in jars and cans in the cellar. Then when the ground is cold, icy, and barren and nothing seems alive, she goes down into the cellar, comes up, and it's May and June at her family's table. How blessed is that person.

I was called back to Oklahoma while in Atlanta. The voice on the phone didn't have to say who she was. She just began by saying, "Ray died." He was a friend of mine in a little church where I had served. It had been years and years and years. We were good friends.

"Ray wanted you to come and have his funeral, if you could." "I'll come," I said.

There was the funeral, where I talked to Mary and the others, and all the family was gathered. The little church in that town gave a fellowship dinner following the funeral. We came from the graveyard to the church, and the women of the church had spread a nice meal. We sat around and talked, and as the peripheral people began to drift away, it left only the family. Kathryn was there. She was the oldest daughter. When I served that church, she was thirteen years old. I remember her when I left, and she was the worst thirteen-year-old I had ever seen. I mean, she was noisy, in and out, pushing, shoving, breaking things, never stayed in the room, out of the room, never paid attention. When I left there, I could have said, "If there's one person that doesn't know a thing I've said in the time I was here, it would be Kathryn."

Kathryn, now an executive with the telephone company, has premature gray sprinkled in her hair. We were sitting at the table talking, and I said, "I'm sorry, it's such a tough time." She and her dad were real close. I said it again.

She said, "It is tough. When Mother called and said Dad had died of a heart attack, I was just scrambling for something. Then I remembered a sermon you had preached on the meaning of the Lord's supper."

I said, "You're kidding, Kathryn," and she told me something I had said in that sermon.

Who knows? Who knows?

Years ago I was a sort of devotional speaker or something for a youth camp in Colorado. Back then we called it a sight-setter. Not a very large camp, I think about sixty, seventy kids. Seemed like five hundred once they got off the bus, just wild and running and everything. But they had a pastor, the chaplain, the director, who just wanted the whole week to be so meaningful for these kids and for the rest of us too. He just kept telling us how meaningful it was. He drove us up the wall. "You know these are really some meaningful trees out here." Just think how meaningful the squirrels are; the pinecones were meaningful; the creeks were meaningful. It was just so meaningful. He told the kids, "You know, Thursday morning we're going to have a special breakfast. It's going to be a meaningful breakfast. We're going to have a breakfast that's going to be just almost like a communion service. It's just going to be so meaningful, you're just going to think we're in church having communion with Jesus by the side of the Sea of Galilee. Thursday morning, the breakfast is really, really going to be meaningful. Remember, Thursday morning breakfast— it's going to be really meaningful."

Thursday morning came, and the kids came in, looking at their shoelaces, sitting down awkwardly. One of the kids dressed up. I mean, this is meaningful. They didn't know what to do. They just sat there and stirred the food in their plates; they didn't know whether to eat. What do you do with meaningful eggs? They just didn't know what to do, it was awkward. So finally somebody got up, and others got up, and they just rushed out. How keenly disappointed the director was. You know what I think—I don't know this—but you know what I think? If he had trusted that what was prayed and sung and said, like a seed that carries its own future in its bosom, if he had just put it out there and left it alone, I daresay that as they loaded the blankets and things into the bus on Saturday, the meanest kid in the group would've said, "You know, this has been more church than church to me."

There was a man from the Agriculture Department in Washington with the Association in one of the regions of the South. The dairymen were complaining about the low price of milk, and the fellow from Washington, D.C., said, "Well, now look, this is a temporary matter, but it all works to your advantage if we can keep the price down low so that marginal dairymen and those who are just starting in the business will have to go out of business. Then it will be left to you, and then you can raise the price. It'll work to your advantage."

Hands went up in the air, and somebody said, "Those marginal dairymen you're talking about—I go to church with them. One of those just getting started is my son-in-law, and I don't appreciate what you've said."

The man from Washington said, "Now don't get sentimental, don't get sentimental. You know what the Bible teaches, 'To them that have, more will be given, and to him that has not, even what he has is taken away.' That's what the Bible says."

I was in Birmingham with a church, and about twelve or thirteen couples asked me on a Tuesday evening to come to a Bible study and prayer in one of the homes. I did, and we didn't really study the Bible; in fact, there was not prayer. There was a listing of answers to prayer. We went around the room, and people gave their answers to prayer. There was a fellow at the dining table with a little computer machine, and he was tallying the answers to prayer. He told me when they had finished that they'd only been meeting, I don't know, five or six months, and they had over twelve hundred on the list. As they went around the room, people talking about what they had gotten through prayer, there was a mink stole, there was new luggage, there was a date with somebody named

Mike, there was a trip to Hawaii, several other nice things like that. In the course of the evening, I said, "I'm a little bothered that these are your prayers in a world anguishing and languishing under oppression and falsehood and poverty and disease, and mink stoles, and rings, and trips, and dates, and…"One of those present said, "Well, Jesus said, 'Whatever you ask I'll give it to you.' It's in the book."

I heard a minister say at the time of the United States' retaliation against Libya, in which one of the children of Gadhafi was killed, this minister said, "Well, we didn't kill old Gadhafi, but at least we got one of his kids."

I said, "Well, whatever you may think of the strike and the good that it'll do, I don't see how anyone can rejoice over the death of a child. It's just a child."

He said, "Well, the Bible says, 'Eye for eye, and tooth for tooth.' It's in the book."

A young woman said to me, during her freshman year of college, "I was a failure in my classes; I wasn't having any dates; and I didn't have as much money as the other students. I was just so lonely and depressed and homesick and not succeeding. One Sunday afternoon," she said, "I went to the river near the campus. I had climbed up on the rail and was looking into the dark water below. For some reason or another I thought of the line, 'Cast all your cares upon him for he cares for you.'" She said, "I stepped back, and here I am."

I said, "Where did you learn that line?"

She said, "I don't know."

I said, "Do you go to church?"

"No…Well, when I visited my grandmother in the summers we went to Sunday school and church."

I said, "Ah…"

Some years ago, some of us who were ministers, pastors, and teachers in seminaries were asked to form a group and, before a large body of students and laypersons, to say who was the most influential person apart from our parents in the formation of our lives and our movement to ministry. We had two or three weeks notice, but it was a difficult matter for me. Finally, when my turn came, I stood up and gave them a name they had never heard of. I said, "Miss Emma Sloan."

As children, we called all women "Miss." Miss Emma Sloan was an elderly woman, single. She taught me in the primary department, and since there was nobody to teach us as juniors, she went right on with us, and taught us for years. She gave me a Bible. She wrote in the front: "May this be a light to your feet, a lamp for your path. Emma Sloan." She taught us to memorize the Bible; she never tried to interpret it. I don't remember her ever explaining anything. She said, "Just put it in your heart, just put it in your heart."

She used the alphabet, and we'd go around the room saying verses. A—A soft answer turns away wrath. B—Be ye kind, one to another, tenderhearted, forgiving each other, as God also in Christ has forgiven you. C—Come unto me, all you who labor and are heavy laden. D—Do unto others as you would have them do unto you. E—Every good and perfect gift…F—For God so loved the world…Don't worry, I'm not going to go on.

I still remember all that. She didn't explain it. We learned from the King James Bible all those verses. I had to say to those students and church folk that Sunday afternoon, "I can't think of anything, anything in all my life that has made such a radical difference as those verses. The Spirit of God brings them to my mind appropriately, time and time and time again."

When I was a kid on the farm, my sister and my brothers and I would play hide-and-seek. We would play that in the country, for it doesn't cost anything. We grew tired of it, but we played it. You remember how it goes. One person is "It." Whoever is "It" hides their eyes, counts to a hundred, and then says, "Coming, ready or not," and you're supposed to be hidden. Then the person who's "It" comes looking and tries to beat the first one found back to the base in order to touch the base three times and say, "You're It." Then the other person is "It."

My sister was "It." When my sister was "It," she cheated. Well, she started off honestly enough; she would say, "One, two, three, four, five, six, seven, ninety-three, ninety-four." But I had a place under the porch and under the steps of the porch. Because of my size I could get under there, and I knew she'd never find me. "Ninety-nine, one hundred. Here I come, ready or not." Here she came, in the house, out of the house, in the weeds, in the trees, down to the corncrib, in the barn. She couldn't find me. I almost gave myself away, down under there just snickering to myself, *She'll never find me here, she'll never find me here.* Then it occurred to me…she'll never find me here. So after awhile I would stick out a toe. When she came by and saw my toe, she said, "Uh oh, I see you," and she'd run back and touch the base three times and say, "Ha ha, you're it, you're it." I would come out brushing myself off saying, "Oh shoot, you found me."

What did I want? What did I really want? The very same thing as you. Isn't that true?

I've told some of my friends what a shocking thing it was to discover that I had not really heard the story of the prodigal son when I preached those sermons about his coming from the far country, about them bringing the ring and the robe and killing the fatted calf. Then they bring the musicians, and there's a party, and there's music and dancing, and all of that. I preached that sermon as though this was the wonderful, natural, easy, right thing to do.

I had never thought about that party until a family up the street divorced and left three or four youngsters, girls, one of them attractive, prematurely mature, and about fourteen years old. She was truant at school, into marijuana, always in trouble, always up before the judge, chasing around and hanging on the tail end of every motorcycle that went roaring through the neighborhood. She finally was so truant and so involved in misdemeanors that the judge said, "You're going to the reform school in southern Oklahoma." She was sent away to a detention home for girls. About the fourth or fifth month that she was there, she gave birth to the child she was carrying. She was fifteen at the time.

Word came to the neighborhood some months afterward that she was coming home. "Will she have that baby with her?" "Is she really coming home, back to our neighborhood?" The day we heard she was to come, all of us in the neighborhood had to mow our grass. We were out in our yards, mowing our grass, and watching the house. She didn't show, nobody came, and we kept watching the house and mowing the grass. I was down to about a blade at a time, you know, watching the house, when a car pulled in the driveway—and out steps... "It's Cathy. She has the baby. She brought home the baby." People in the house ran out and grabbed her and took turns holding that baby, and they were all laughing and joking, then they went in. Another car pulled in, then another car pulled in, and another car pulled in. They started parking in the street. You couldn't have gotten a Christian car down the street, just cars on either side, and they're all gathering there, you know. Suddenly I got disturbed and anxious and went in my house. It suddenly struck me, what if one of them saw me down in the yard and said, "Hey Fred, she's home and she has the baby. We're giving a party, and we'd like for you and Nettie to come."

"Well, I've got a lot of papers to grade and all." Would I have gone? If you lived next door to the prodigal son's father's house, would you have gone over to the party? It's easier to preach on that than to go to the party.

I remember one night, sitting in a little rural church on a Sunday night. It was a summer meeting, so it was hot, and the window was open beside my pew. The minister was preaching on his favorite text, "Be not the first by whom the new is tried, because a bird in the hand is worth two in the bush, and it's better to be safe than sorry, because fools rush in where angels fear to tread."

I was listening to him drone away when a man came by the church building and stopped by the window and said, "Psst, psst."

I said, "What is it? I'm listening to the sermon."

He said, "Come with me."

I said, "Where are you going?"

He said, "I know where there is a pearl of great price that's more valuable than all the other pearls in the world."

I said, "There's no such thing."

He said, "In fact, where I'm going, there is treasure buried in a field."

I said, "You're kidding!"

He said, "Where I'm going, bums are invited to sit down at the king's table."

I said, "That's ridiculous."

He said, "In fact, they give great big parties for prodigals who come home."

I said, "That's stupid." Well, I listened to the rest of the sermon and after it was over, I told the preacher about how I was disturbed and that I hoped it didn't upset him during the sermon.

He said, "Who was that?"

I said, "I don't know. Telling me all this fancy stuff."

He said, "Well, was he getting anybody?"

And I said, "Well, none of our crowd went, but I noticed he had about twelve with him."

Some time ago, I was out in the yard and saw a sparrow walking down the street. Weighed about nine pounds, I guess. I said, "What are you doing walking?"

He said, "I'm trying to get some of this weight off."

I said, "Well, I noticed you're kind of heavy. Why don't you fly?"

He said, "Fly?"

I said, "Yeah, why don't you fly?"

He said, "Are you crazy? I've never flown before."

I said, "Really? What is your name?"

And he said, "Fred."

I went a couple of years ago to the house where Faith was born. I don't know if any of you have been there. There's a little marker there, but it's off on a side road, and it's hard to find. I was really disappointed at first because the house where Faith was born, I thought, would be a sort of castle, with a spire maybe, soft music, carpets, and a little guest book to sign. It wasn't. You know, I thought, maybe it'll be a study, with all the walls lined with great books of great preachers and theologians and biblical scholars, the house where Faith was born. But when I got there, that was not it at all.

It was a farmhouse. The father said at breakfast one morning to his son, "When the calf is born, it'll be yours."

"Mine? You mean it'll be all mine? You don't mean mine and my sisters, but just mine? It'll be all mine?"

"Yes, sir, you can take care of it and groom it and name it. It's all yours; it's up to you and then you can keep it, sell it, whatever."

"It's all mine?"

"Yeah."

"Well, I want to stay home from school."

"Well, it's not going to be born today. You go on to school."

"But I don't want to."

"Go on to school."

Finally, one day at breakfast the father said, "I think today's the day."

"I want to stay home from school."

"No, you go on to school. I don't know what time…"

"I'm not going to listen."

"I know you're not, but go on to school."

Finally he got on the school bus and went away to school. It took an eternity to get out, but finally the school bus comes back, he dashes off the bus and onto the back porch, throws down the books, and runs out to the stall. In the barn there's the big brown-eyed cow standing knee-deep in that glistening golden straw, and down beneath her in the straw, a two-headed dead calf.

The little boy goes to church with momma and daddy the next Sunday, and the preacher says, "God loves us and cares for us." But my calf is dead. "God is alive in Jesus Christ and has raised Jesus from the dead and has given us all new hope." But my calf is dead. And the child sits there, pressed against momma and daddy. How can he believe? I don't want a preacher telling me it's as plain as the nose on my face. My calf is dead.

A colleague of mine down at Phillips University, a young woman, taught physical education. She was a marvelous person, young, vigorous, unmarried. One night she was sitting in her apartment grading papers, and she heard a knock at the door. She went to the door, unlocked it, opened it, and there stood death, with his yellow face staring right at her. She slammed the door, locked it, and called the doctor. He said, "Malignant." She had surgery. A few months later she was back, and I said, "Hey, you're looking good." She said, "I never felt better." Now, she had lost some weight, but she was back teaching physical education, bouncing on trampolines and all, doing great. Everything seemed to be wonderful.

She was at home one night watching television when she heard a knock at the door. She went to the door, opened it, and there he stood with his yellow face. She slammed it and locked it and called the doctor. He said, "Chemotherapy." Oh, she was sick. All her hair came out, so she got a wig, and she came back to school. I said, "That's becoming. You should've been wearing that all along." She said, "I feel pretty good." And she was teaching again.

One night she was sitting there grading papers in her room, and she heard a knock, so she went to the door, unlocked it, and there he stood, old death with his yellow face. She slammed the door and tried to lock it, but the lock was broken. She called her friends and relatives. Everybody gathered, and we took turns leaning against that door. We leaned against the door; we leaned against the door. We even got to where we were joking and laughing, "We're not going to let him in. We'll keep him out." We'd look out the window, and there he sat under a tree with his yellow face right out there.

One night she said, "Get away from the door."

"What?"

"Get away from the door." So we got away from the door, and he came in. I felt sorry for him. He likes to come in with his fiery darts of pain and fear. There he stood; in one hand he had peace, in the other, rest. He looked like a servant of God.

Oh, I know there are people who say, "Well, it's too bad you lost your friend," and it's true. But I heard the whisper in there as we gathered at the church a couple of days later and the congregation stood in great throng and sang "Now Thank We All Our God." It was a shouted whisper.

I recall once in Israel, being in Bethlehem and having a Jewish man explain the Christmas story to me. He explained this to me when we were standing in Shepherd's Field. Now, some of you may know what I'm talking about. There is a field down in the lower part where there were once tents. Now I think there's a housing development, but nothing sacred anymore. On a clear night if you stand down there and, looking toward the city, you look up, there is a bright star, and it looks like it's standing right over the houses. And that's what happened at Christmas. Of course, he was mixing Matthew and Luke; he was not really an expert in all this. He explained that this is how people got confused and thought there was a star over the house where Jesus was. When he finished, I said, "Well, that's one way to look at it."

Then he said something very interesting. He said, "I know that's just one way to look at it. When I was in school, the rabbi explained everything in the Bible two different ways. When he would come to a miracle, he would explain it two different ways, and his reason was this: If something happens and you can't explain it another way, then God didn't do it."

That's not bad. God does not paint you into a corner and say, "Now, you weasel, you don't have a choice," so that the weasel will say, "I don't have a choice, I believe."

There's always an alternate route if one chooses not to believe. And some do, of course.

I recall once on a plane on a flight to Denver, I was seated in the no smoking section, as is my custom. I was seated on the aisle, and across from me was a man who pulled a long black cigar out of his pocket. You're not supposed to smoke at all on a plane, much less cigars, and he had one of those long black ones made out of gunpowder and gunnysack and stuff. He lit that thing up and was filling the plane with smoke, so I stopped the flight attendant, in this case a very attractive young woman, and I said, "Am I in the wrong section? I asked for no smoking."

She replied, "This is no smoking," and then said to him, "Uh, sir, this is no smoking." He didn't say a word; he went right on. She went on down the aisle to attend to other matters, and when she came back, I said, "He's still smoking. It's terrible here." She said to him, "Sir, you're not even supposed to smoke cigarettes, here, you're not…this is the no smoking…you should be in the smoking section." He didn't even stop, just went right on. I was boiling mad.

So later on, when we got out over the Rocky Mountains, she was coming down the aisle with a tray of pop and things, and we hit turbulence over the mountains, as frequently is the case. She was just between us when, I don't know, we hit air pockets or whatever the term is, and she went over with those drinks, and they went into his lap. Then, in an effort to correct herself, she fell back into my lap. Now, don't tell me there's no God. Once in a while you have an experience where you say, *Now, it's so obvious*. God really shouted there.

I recall once playing in town with a friend of mine when I saw something I'd never seen before. It was tracing paper. I was fascinated by this thin paper, as the only paper I'd had was big, thick tablets of typing paper. The fellow gave me a couple of sheets of it, and I went home and took a catalog, and I took my pencil and traced horses and clothes and all kinds of things. Then when I removed it from the book, there it was, just as pretty as you please—a horse.

I took that tracing paper to my school. I was in first or second grade, and my teacher was going up and down the aisles seeking who she could devour. She paused by my desk and said, "Oh! You're an artist!" Well, I mean, she said it, didn't she? I said, "Well, after a fashion."

Next she said, "We're getting ready for parents' visitation and open house, and we're going to be putting things up around on the walls, on the windows. Now the others are doing the usual, you know, pumpkins and turkeys and pilgrims. Why don't you do some artwork, and we'll put it up? While the others are working on other things, you can work on this."

I worked and worked, and at the close of the day I was still on the first one. She came by and said, "What's the matter?" I told her the truth, and she chastened me a bit. Have you ever done that? Have you ever taken a piece of tracing paper and laid it over Acts 2 and thought it was your sermon?

My wife and I have a friend who is a nurse in a tuberculosis hospital. She resigned the other day. She has fellows in there with one lung, half of one lung, or less; little bitty guys lying up in bed. At night, sometimes with nothing but pajamas and robes on, they tie sheets together and sneak out through a window, door, or any way; go to a liquor store; get all liquored up; and come back in the chill of the night, wheezing and coughing. She gets the oxygen, she nurses them, she goes over another eight-hour shift. She's a beautiful woman, but her legs have those big knotted veins from standing sixteen hours to bring this little frail fellow back to breathing again. Finally it clears up. He's breathing again; she takes away the oxygen; and he ties the sheets together and goes out the window to the liquor store.

And she quits. Why should I care? He doesn't care! Let him die.

The next morning she goes to work.

Especially when I've come to a new insight, and suddenly my life is entirely different, if I'm not careful, I attack people who are like I used to be. I made that mistake in the days of the civil rights movement in the South. I am from western Tennessee. I grew up in prejudice, strong, bitter prejudice. It was a part of my life. I recall once, I was maybe ten years old, my Uncle Jim and I and Will, a friend of mine, were hauling loose hay to the farm. I was up on top of the stack. My Uncle Jim was driving the team of horses. Will, my friend, who was an elderly black man, was sitting on the gate of the wagon. He was my friend; we played together. He was, I guess, eighty years old. He taught me things I never learned in school. He taught me, for instance, how to tell if a watermelon is ripe by putting a broom straw on it. If it turns around, it's ripe. He taught me, for instance, why grapevines are scared and have to hang on to trees. He was a marvelous friend of mine. We were going to the barn, and he said something to me. I didn't hear him, but I knew he'd said something. I just yelled back, "Sir?"

My next conscious moment was looking up from under the front wheel of the wagon, my face half paralyzed from the blow that my uncle had struck, and his bitter face in mine saying, "Boy, if I ever hear you call a nigger 'Sir' again, I'll kill you, so help me, God." And that was the basic training for the minister of the gospel.

Finally, by the good graces of God, I was able to move past that. I became mad at everybody who was prejudiced. Then one day my wife reminded me that I was more prejudiced against the prejudiced than the prejudiced were prejudiced.

I was at a high school football game one night in our town, and there was a lull in the action while they were taking out some of the bodies and putting in other bodies. A woman sitting three or four rows up above in the stands yelled down, "Fred! I was telling my friend here of what you said in that sermon Sunday and that story you were telling, and I've forgotten the punch line of it. Would you tell her how that story went?" I had preached in her church the Sunday before and, in the context of prayer and music and singing and reading of scripture and praise, I had shared a word. She wanted me to yell it up several rows over popcorn and hot dogs and beer. I said, "I'm sorry, I cannot."

I'll be honest with you. I have heard profanity in the street, and I have read profanity on public restroom walls, but I know of no profanity lower than screaming over hot dogs and beer the word that was nestled in the sanctuary.

The minister called on your church and was thrilled to death. The van unloaded him at the parsonage. The chairperson of the pulpit committee had him and his family over in their backyard as they cooked hamburgers. The women filled the pantry with food; the men put in the furniture. It was great. They stood around the barbecue grill, and the young pastor said, "You can't imagine what a delight it is to come to a church and know that you've been elected and chosen to come by unanimous vote."

The fellow flipping the hamburgers said, "Well, it was practically unanimous."

"Well, what do you mean, 'practically unanimous'?"

"Well, it was practically unanimous."

"Well, what do you mean, 'practically unanimous'?"

"Well, let's just say that it was unanimous."

"Well, but what…what was it really?"

"Well, it was 234 to 2."

To two? I wonder who the two are? The next six months he spends finding out who the two are, and then the next six months trying to please those two. At the end of the year, he is fired—2 in favor of him, 234 against.

I remember some years ago being in Florida to speak to a group. It was hot, and I was in a little, sticky hotel somewhere near Ocala, I think it was near Ocala. Now, I can't stand for air conditioning to be blowing right on me, and it was right by the bed. If you didn't hold the sheet down, it just blew the sheet against the wall. I knew I was going to get all crouped up with that, so I turned it off, and then I was sweltering. So I turned it on but moved to the other side of the bed, a little bit away from it. The next morning I got up, and as I was dressing I noticed that I slept part of the night here and part of the night there. I thought, *Now the maid is going to think I was not here alone,* so I started straightening out the bed on one side. Then I found myself thinking, *What do I care about what the maid, well, if some unknown maid…what about my friends, my peers?*

When I was still in Oklahoma, I was asked by one of the people in the development office if I would talk to a man who had lots of money and was interested in improving the quality of the preaching in the church. He did not belong to my church, but he had money and you kind of forget…You become ecumenical when you're after the money, you see. He had a lot of money, and he was growling around about the church needing to improve the teaching and preaching and all.

Development said, "Would you go talk to him?"

I said, "Yeah, make the appointment," and they made the appointment. I arrived to find him rushing out the door and saying, "I've got to make a trip. Why don't you just go with me?"

I said, "Where are you going?"

He said, "I have to go out to one of my ranches."

So I said, "All right." I thought it was down the road. We went out to a little airstrip, a pilot and plane waiting. We got on the plane and zoom. We landed at another airstrip in about forty-five minutes, where there was a car and somebody waiting. I thought, *My land, I'm in the tall cotton here. This is big stuff.* We started out early, it was the early morning, in the spring, late March, early April, and it was damp and cool. We started driving down through these fields, fields of green. Winter wheat was coming up, and the cattle were on it. Black angus cattle as far as you could see, and he was saying, "This is mine, and this is mine, and this is mine, and this is mine." I didn't mind because I wanted to go home saying, "This is mine."

We drove up to this rural farmhouse, a fairly large old house, and I said, "It's almost lunchtime, I don't like to go to someone's house at lunch." He said, "That's all right; we'll eat with them. That's where my manager lives." We got there, and a man named Clyde something came out. I shook his hand, they talked, we went inside. As we went inside the house, I saw to the left what was the den or living room with a huge stone fireplace. Someone, a woman, had just put on the largest—I guess three-foot-long—piece of wood on the fire. Clyde said, "Just go in and warm yourself." I went in, backed up to the fire, and they talked cattle. They talked cattle for quite awhile. After a while I heard a door creak just a little bit, then Clyde said to me, "Well, lunch is ready, let's go eat."

We went into what was really the kitchen, the eating area, and just as we did I saw the back of a woman move out of the room. The three of us ate, lots of good country food and milk and apple pie—very good. Clyde said, "Well, might as well go back to the fire." As we turned to go back to the fire, I saw the back of a woman putting another log on the fire and then disappearing down another way. I don't know who she was. I warmed myself awhile, and then I thought, I'm going to go see who that is. I went to the door, into where we had been eating, and there she sat with her back to me. Little gray clump of hair, and she was eating by herself. I wanted to go in and say, "Can I have another cup of coffee?" and just sit with her, I mean, she's eating by herself. The three of us had eaten, and now she's eating by herself. But I knew that if I walked in there and said, "Can I have another cup of coffee?" she'd have gotten up with her plate and said, "Sure, I was through anyway."

I knew what she would do. I didn't know what to do. I just didn't do anything. They got through talking cattle, then he said, "Time to go." I said, "Okay, but I'd like to thank the lady for the excellent lunch."

"I'll tell her," Clyde said.

I said, "Well, I would like to thank her."

"I'll tell her you liked it."

I said, "All right." We started out to the car, and I said to my host, "I would like to have thanked the lady for the fine meal."

"Clyde'll tell her."

I said, "Well, it really was a good meal."

He said, "Yeah, she's a good cook."

I said, "Who is she?"

He said, "That's Clyde's wife."

I said, "What's her name?"

And he said, "Uh, uh, uh, I think her name is Ruth." Clyde's been managing his place seventeen years, and he thinks her name is Ruth?

There is a church in Georgia where the chairman of the board proposed at the annual meeting that they have keys made and give each family a key to the church. They should otherwise keep it locked because, he said, "You don't know who can come in the church."

I mean, how are you going to have family if you don't make it clear who's not family? No shoes, no shirt, no service.

I preached four nights in a church in Atlanta, a nice, big church with a good crowd, more than I'm used to. There was a moment in the service in which the pastor said, "We'll now have our moments of fellowship. Greet each other in Christian love," and you never saw such hugging and kissing and carrying on in your life—people going across the room, and up and down the aisles, and grabbing and hugging. Somebody came up to me—I was down behind the pulpit—and gave me a big smack. It was just really something. Finally he said, "All right, hold it, hold it. We have to get on with the worship." Four nights of that.

The last night, he and his wife took me and my wife out to coffee. He said, "Did you ever see such a family church? Did you ever see such love in your life in a church?"

My wife said, "Yeah, well, yeah, I have."

He said, "What do you mean?"

She said, "I was there for all four services, and nobody ever spoke to me."

And do you know what he said? He said, "Well, that was because they didn't know who you were."

My wife was away some time ago, and I was going to fix one of my big meals. I stopped off at the Winn Dixie to get a jar of peanut butter. I was in a hurry, and those stores are just so huge, and who wants to spend the afternoon looking around? So I saw a woman who was pushing a cart in a kind of stroll, and I thought, *She's comfortable here. I'll ask her.* I said, "Um, lady, could you direct me to the peanut butter?"

She jerked around, stared at me, and said, "Are you trying to hit on me?"

I said, "I'm looking for the peanut butter." As I backed away from there I saw a stock boy, so I said, "Where's the peanut butter?"

"Aisle five, I think, way down on the left."

I went down there, and halfway down on the left were big jars of peanut butter. I took one. As I turned to leave, that woman was there and she said, "You *were* looking for the peanut butter!"

I said, "I told you I was looking for the peanut butter."

She said, "Well, nowadays you can't be too careful."

And I said, "Lady, yes you can. Yes you can."

You don't just turn loose of life. Life is a very tenacious thing and will not give itself up easily. First time I ever realized that was while chopping cotton on a farm. I don't know if you know what chopping cotton is, but you're chopping everything but the cotton. You're chopping the weeds and all. But there was a snake, which I killed, but then I had to keep chopping the snake, calling my father and saying, "I've killed the snake, but it won't quit wiggling."

He said, "Well, son, a snake won't die until sundown." I didn't know that. He said, "You hang it on a fence," so I picked it up with a hoe and put it over on a fence. Every once in a while I'd look over at the fence, and there was just the tail of that snake moving just like that, until sundown. I learned for the first time that it's hard to give up life, just turn it loose.

And Jesus said, "I'm going to turn it loose." But it was not a decision that was determined by his friends—they tried to oppose it—and it was not a decision determined by his enemies. He looked at them with a level gaze and said, "You're not taking my life; I'm giving my life." He was free.

Our family, having lost the farm, had moved into town, and I wasn't accustomed to it. The isolation of the farm had made me rather socially inadequate, retarded I suppose. We dressed in what was given to us by charitable organizations, and I went to school. The first day of school the teacher announced, "Let's get acquainted and start our school year by everybody telling what you did on vacation." I was off to a bad start. It was unbelievable. I was darning a knot in the back of the room, and here these other boys and girls told of what their families had done together on vacation. I remember there was a girl who reported that they had spent a week in Florida. Another had gone to Niagara Falls. These are pictures in books, and they had gone there. Someone else reported that their family had gone to Washington and seen all the historical monuments and all that. I was at the back, and she would get to me pretty soon. What was I going to say? When you work on a farm all summer, what do you say? Well, everybody else had such marvelous vacations. She didn't get to me. She said, "We'll continue tomorrow."

So I went home, and my father saw I was worried and said, "What's the matter?"

I said, "It didn't go well today."

He said, "What's the matter?"

I said, "The teacher wants us all to tell what we did on vacation, and I just, you know, dug potatoes and picked and shelled purple-hulled peas and things like that. I don't have anything to tell."

He said, "She asked you what? What you did on vacation? Obviously, your teacher is asking you for a lie, so you give her one."

"But you and Mama have told us that we're not supposed to lie."

He said, "Son, you're supposed to obey your teacher."

"But what am I going to say?"

He said, "Well, just pick the good parts out of several others and put it together, and you'll be all right."

So when she got to me, I started to tie them on. "I went up to New York and Washington…" I was somewhere on this side of Niagara Falls when she called me into the hall. She said, "You didn't do all that."

I said, "No, ma'am."

"Well, why then did you say that?"

I said, "Because I was embarrassed."

"Why were you embarrassed?"

I said, "I worked on the farm all summer."

She stopped the proceeding. If I had thought, if I knew then what I know now, I would've told the boys and girls what I did that summer, and I would've been the envy of everybody. I don't know if you know anything about sweet potatoes, but when sweet potatoes are at a certain stage of growth, they're just kind of a long bulb with a long tail, the root. You can take one by the tail and you can knock a squirrel off a limb, or even better you can send your sister screaming to the house. I should've told them that, but I didn't. I didn't tell that.

There was a group of women from what was called the Ladies' Aid Society of Central Avenue Christian Church in Humboldt, Tennessee, that brought a box of things for children to wear. There was a pair of Buster Brown shoes in the box that were my size.

My mother said, "Good, you will go to Sunday school on Sunday." I didn't want to go to Sunday school because I figured it would be the same: What did you do on vacation? But from that first day, wearing those charity shoes that I found out later were really girls' shoes, I was never, ever embarrassed in church. I don't remember ever feeling any different, any less, any more, any different from anybody else in church. And from the age of nine until now, I have had this little jubilee going on in my mind: There is no place in the world like church.

I remember the first church I served as a student. They had a fund called the Emergency Fund and had about $100 in it. They told me I could use it at my discretion, provided I dispensed the money according to the conditions. So I said, "What are the conditions?"

The chairman of the committee said, "You are not to give the money to anybody who is in need as a result of laziness, drunkenness, or poor management."

I said, "Well, what else is there?" Far as I know, they still have that money.

I was in graduate school at Vanderbilt. I had left the family and children in the little parish I served and moved into a little room to prepare for those terrible comprehensive exams. It's make-it-or-break-it time; they can kill you. I would go every night about 11:30 or 12:00 to a little all-night diner—no tables, just little stools—and have a grilled cheese and a cup of coffee to take a break from my studies. It was the same every night; the fellow behind the counter at the grill knew when I walked in to prepare a grilled cheese and a cup of coffee. He'd give me a refill, sometimes come again and give me another refill. I joined the men of the night sitting there hovering over coffee, still thinking about my own possible questions about the New Testament oral exams.

Then I noticed a man who was there when I went in, but had not yet been waited on. I had been waited on, had a refill, and so had the others. Then finally the man behind the counter went to the man at the end of the counter and said, "What do you want?" He was an old, gray-haired, black man. Whatever the man said, the fellow went to the grill, scooped up a little dark patty off the back of the grill, and put it on a piece of bread without condiment, without napkin. The cook handed it to the man, who gave him some money, and then went out the side door by the garbage can and out on the street. He sat on the curb with the eighteen-wheelers of the night with the salt and pepper from the street to season his sandwich.

I didn't say anything. I did not reprimand, protest, or witness to the cook. I did not go out and sit beside the man on the curb, on the edge. I didn't do anything. I was thinking about the questions coming up on the New Testament. And I left the little place, went up the hill back to my room to resume my studies, and off in the distance I heard a cock crow.

I was in a distant city, and the seminar in which I was involved ended on Saturday at lunch. Our host had insisted if we could possibly stay over on Sunday, it would help our budget because the airlines give a big break if you stay over Saturday night. I could and did, but the little motel where I was housed did not seem to be in a church district. I asked at the counter on Sunday morning, "Is there a church near here to which I could walk?"

After a little huddle behind the counter they said, "Well, there's one about three or four blocks down this way," pointing in one direction.

I said, "Do you know what kind it is?"

They said, "No, we don't know."

I said, "That's okay." So I walked and I went in. It was a small building, modestly built, one of those that looks like the men of the church helped build it, because they seemed to love it very much. It was warm and friendly, not elaborate at all for worship. I took my seat, a bit early, but it soon began to fill up and soon was totally filled. I would say there were about 120 people. At the appointed hour, the choir came down. Following the choir came the minister, in this case, a man.

I was absolutely shocked. He was very tall—I forgave him for that. I suppose he was 6'4". He was also very large, maybe 280 or 300 pounds. But the most noticeable feature was his stumbling, lumbering gait. He was awkward, almost falling, with his long useless arms at his sides, like they were awaiting further instruction. His head was misshapen, his hair was askew. He stumbled up the three or four steps to get to the pulpit. When he turned to face us, I saw the thick glasses, and through them I could see the milky film over his eyes, one of his eyes going out, nothing coming in to the other. When he read, he held the book near his nose. When he spoke, the sinews of his neck worked with such vigor as he pushed out the words, it was as if he had learned to speak as an adult. But I lost all consciousness of that after a while. He read 1 Corinthians 13 and spoke on the subject in the bulletin, "But the greatest of these is love." It was an unusual thing. If you had a copy of his sermon, you would say, I'd give it a grade of "C." It was not poetic, it was not prophetic, it was pastoral. It was so warm and so full of love and affection. It was firm, and it had exhortation in it. But the relationship between those people, the love that he extended as he preached, and the love that came back from those people who sat quietly, leaning forward, was captivating, and I was captured. What is this? How could this grotesque creature be so full of love? I didn't understand. I started remembering things that I shouldn't have remembered—all those stories about how people who have grotesque features sometimes are granted a special quality of affection, *Beauty and the Beast* or Victor Hugo's *Hunchback of Notre Dame*, so ugly and yet so beautiful in his love and capacity for affection. I thought of children with Down's Syndrome, how they have the capacity to love and grab you and hug you and kiss you, when other children stand at a distance. Is this what I'm seeing here? The providence of God that grants people who lack the attractiveness on the outside to have that quality on the inside?

I wanted to get acquainted with this extraordinary preacher, so I lingered at the door hoping to invite him to lunch. He couldn't go, but as I stood at the door and observed the greetings and hellos and little words of pastoral care, comfort, and respect between him and the members, one woman I would guess to be seventy shook his hand at the door. She spoke with him and said this: "I wish I could know your mother." I saw her having the same trouble as I was. She didn't understand the source of this and thought maybe, *I wish I knew your mother.* He said, "My mother's name is Grace."

When everybody had left and I began to visit with him, we sat on the back pew for a few minutes, and I said, "That was an unusual response you gave to that woman, 'My mother's name is Grace.'"

And he said, "It is? When I was born," he said, "I was put up for adoption at the Department of Family Services. But as you can see, nobody wanted to adopt me. So I went from foster home to foster home, and when I was about sixteen or seventeen, I saw some young people going into a church. I wanted to be with young people, so I went in, and there I met grace—the grace of God."

⸱⸱═◦⊹◦═⸱⸱

It is not with the blink of the eye that a thirty-something year old will say to me, "Let's see now, was it next Sunday that my daughter was going to be baptized?"

I said, "Yeah, next Sunday."

"Well...she has dance lessons next Sunday."

I said, "Well, this is Sunday morning."

"Well...the dance lessons are at 10:30."

"On Sunday morning?"

"Yeah. The dance studio has classes on Sunday morning."

I said, "On *Sunday* morning?" That's what she said, Sunday morning. I said, "Then we have a decision to make, don't we?"

I preached in Blue Ridge, the little town near where I live and where I get my mail. I actually live at Cherry Log but I go into Blue Ridge for the mail because, well, we have a post office at Cherry Log, but our mule died, and it's just hand-delivered now, so it takes longer. So I preached in Blue Ridge while the minister was away, and I preached on the lectionary text for that Sunday, which was the prodigal son. I preached on the prodigal son. A man after the service said, "I really didn't care much for that, frankly."

I said, "Why?"

He said, "Well, I guess it's not your sermon, I just don't like that story."

I said, "What is it you don't like about it?"

He said, "It's not morally responsible."

I said, "What do you mean by that?"

"Forgiving that boy."

I said, "Well, what would you have done?"

He said, "I think when he came home he should've been arrested."

This fellow was serious. *He's an attorney,* I thought. I thought he was going to tell me a joke. But he was really serious. He belonged to this unofficial organization nationwide, never has any meetings and doesn't have a name, but it's a very strong network that I call "quality control people." They're the moral police. Mandatory sentences and no parole, mind you, and executions.

I said, "What would you have given the prodigal?"

He said, "Six years."

Once in Bluefield, West Virginia, in the absence of a minister, I had a funeral for a seventeen year-old boy who was killed in a car wreck. As it turned out, he was one of eleven children. The other ten, healthy and happy, surrounded their mother, who was a widow. She screamed out several times at the church and then twice again at the graveyard: "If I'd have known this was going to happen, I'd never have had any children!"

And there are ten children looking at her. It hurt me, so I got them together and I said, "Now, your mother's distraught. She doesn't really mean that."

But one of them said to me, "Yes, she does. But if I were the one who was killed, she would've said that too."

I recall a fellow who was always sitting in the front row looking up at me through an entire semester study on the book of Galatians. It's only six chapters, but we spent the semester on it. It's a difficult book, a difficult letter. Paul is angered to begin with, so we had to deal with that; we struggled a lot. I couldn't understand why this fellow in the front row sat there smiling, with a kind of beatific face, while we were struggling with law and gospel. At the close of the semester he came up and thanked me. He said, "You know, I think you can just sum up that whole book in one point."

I said, "What's that?"

"If you hold him up, he won't let you down."

I said, "Well…um…I thank you for that, but…that's not going to be on the test."

I recall preaching in a university church in Norman, Oklahoma, some years ago, when a young woman came up after the service. I had preached on Mark 1, the call of the disciples. She came up and said she wanted to talk with me and said, "I'm in med school here, and that sermon clinched what I've been struggling with for some time."

"What's that?"

"Dropping out of med school."

"What do you want to do that for?"

She said she was going to go work in the Rio Grande Valley. She said, "I believe that's what God wants me to do." She quit med school, went to the Rio Grande Valley, sleeps under a piece of tin in the back of a pickup truck, and teaches little children while their parents are out in the field. She dropped out of med school for this, and her folks back in Montana are saying, "What in the world happened?"

And I was saying to her, "Well, now, I was just preaching, I didn't mean to, you know."

⊷⇒✦⇐⊶

U sed to have a kid down home who'd believe anything you'd tell him. You could say, "The schoolhouse burned down. We're not having school tomorrow."

"Oh boy!" He'd believe it.

"They're giving away free watermelons down at the town hall."

"Really? Free watermelons?" He'd go running off.

"Did you know the president of the United States is coming to our town tomorrow?"

"He is? Really? Whoopee!" He just believed everything.

I remember once there was an evangelist who came to our town, and he said to that kid, "God loves you and cares for you and comes to you in Jesus Christ." And do you know, that kid believed it? He actually believed it.

⊷⇒✦⇐⊶

W hen I was in the pastorate in Columbia, Tennessee, there was a fellow who played golf on Sunday mornings. He was a member of our church; he was on the board. He would call me on Sunday afternoons and say, "You know what my score was?" Now my plan was, and I clearly explained it to God, for him to have terrible scores on Sunday mornings, but he would call me up and say, "Number three, birdie; number four, birdie; number five…"

I said, "You're lying."

He said, "No, it's true, I have witnesses."

So I said to God, "If you would make him shoot about 108 every Sunday morning, pretty soon he would be in church. Let the rain come right up to the fence, let the sun shine right up to the fence. I believe in those old slogans. Teach him a lesson. Let's take a stand." And God sends the sun and the rain upon the just and the unjust, where there is no distinction.

When I was in high school in summer conference, we used to have what was called CWFF, the Christian World Friendship Fund. Any of you remember that? Man, we'd steal and embezzle and everything to put money in that pot. We really had a good fund. We had 140-something dollars. After the closing, you know, the consecration service and candlelight and night of silence and all, we were going to decide what to do with this money. There had been a natural disaster in some foreign place, I don't know, a tidal wave, an earthquake, some terrible thing, and we were deciding whether or not we wanted to send our money there. Well, it looked like a great thing to do and it looked like it was going to carry, when somebody said, "Is that country Communist?"

Well, we didn't know. One of the counselors said, "Well, it's pretty heavily communistic, but I don't know what percentage."

"Well, then I don't think we ought to send it there."

Somebody said, "Well, look, these babies don't know whether they're Communists or not. All they know is that they're hungry."

"But, no, we just can't do that."

"Well, how do we know?"

"We don't know. We've got to be careful, right?"

"You feed them today, you fight them tomorrow, right?"

Finally, after an hour of arguing, the vote was taken. We spent the 140-something dollars to improve the recreational facilities at our campground.

When a colleague in ministry with a terminal disease knew that his hour had approached, he called me into his study and said, "I have something to show you."

I said, "What is it?"

He said, "Come on in here," so I went into the study. He handed me an order of worship. I looked at it and said, "What's this?"

He said, "This is the way I'd like my funeral to be. I love these songs and these scriptures and all." I said, "Oh, Bob, my goodness."

"Yeah, yeah, yeah, yeah. We've worked it out, my wife and I."

It seemed morbid to me; it was heavy, and I couldn't shake it off. A few days later, there we were going through the order of worship. When the congregation stood to sing "Now Thank We All Our God," in came his widow, wearing a red hat. Can you believe it?

Some time ago, following a service of worship in which I had been asked to preach at this little church, I was invited by this lady to lunch. She was a widow and was alone. We went into the house, and she said, "Go into the den and read the paper or watch TV. I'll have it ready in a minute." She put on her apron, and she busied herself in the dining room. I saw where she'd gone, so I went in there and said, "Now, don't fix up all this. We eat in the kitchen at home." She pulled out a drawer of that big thing in the dining room, a buffet or a sideboard, whatever you call it. She took out linens, linen napkins. She put the cloth on, the napkins on, and then opened that beautiful case with the curved glass and took out stemmed glasses. She wiped the dust out, and I said, "We eat in the kitchen at home." She went right on. I said, "Look, I mean it's just the two of us. We eat in the kitchen at home."

She turned around and with level gaze said to me, "Will you shut up and sit down?"

I said, "Well, I suppose I will."

She said, "Do you have any idea what it's like fixing a meal for one?" And we ate in the dining room with stemmed glasses and candles and linens.

There was a man on our street, Mr. Hill. He was an old man who used to walk his dog by the house. The dog was as old as he was, and they shuffled along with painful steps. The little dog had a harness and a leash. The leash was not to control the dog but to find it. And every afternoon, Mr. Hill shuffled along by. One day my wife said, "Mr. Hill hasn't been by this afternoon."

I said, "Oh, you probably missed him."

The next afternoon, she said, "I'm afraid he's sick." So the next afternoon when I came in, she said, "I want you to take this down and see Mr. Hill." She had made a pie she calls the Million Dollar Pie. That used to be the name of it; now it's the price of it. And she gave me one and said, "Take this down there and see. I'm afraid he's ill."

He was not ill, but I discovered what the problem was. When I went inside the door, I saw the little harness that had been on the dog hanging on a nail. We visited a little bit. He was alone. He belongs to one of our churches in town, a nice church with a nice pastor and a lot of nice members. And he is a member of that church. When I got back home, I asked Nettie, "What's he being punished for? I never see anybody there. I never see any cars. I never see anybody come from the church. What's he being punished for?"

And she said, "You see, what he did was he got old."

I said, "Oh."

Now, Ms. Patterson, she's being punished. She lives at the Sunset Home; it's a nice place and well-landscaped. Inside are all the things you need, large-print Bibles, stainless steel trays, and some checkerboards. You can look out of her window to some black asphalt with those lines painted on it at a slant. I suppose you could get seventy-five or eighty cars on that lot. And it has a big sign out there, "Reserved for Visitors." She can read that sign and look out and count all the lines on the carless lot.

I asked one of the women on the CWF, "What's she in for?"

The lady said to me, "They found her talking to herself."

I said, "Oh...Give her enough of that and she'll repent."

When I had the flu last winter, I was at home five days. I looked out the window and watched Mrs. Gower go out for her mail. She'd go out and raise the lid of this little metal box and forage around inside. Then she would go back inside and get a little stool, because she is one of those delightful people who is the right size. She would step up on the stool because sometimes in the mailbox you get those little bitty cards, you know, those little notes from people, and you don't see them through the little slot. So she would reach more deeply into the box and forage about. Sometimes the postman would stop and flip through his bundle and shake his head. And I watched out...five days I was confined to bed, five days he shook his head, five days she stood on her stool. I thought, *Boy, they're punishing her.*

I asked her pastor at the ministerial alliance, "What'd she do wrong?"

He said, "Arthritis. She wasn't able to get up the church steps."

I said, "Oh."

When we were in Europe, in Germany, studying for a year, I'd been down to Zurich in Switzerland, several days from my family in another country. I was overwhelmed with a sense of melancholy. I was lonely. I got on the train and grabbed a sandwich. On the German trains I would usually try to get a place in a compartment where there were already several people so I could just be at the fringe of the conversation. My German was not very good. I mean, how many times can you say, "auf Wiedersehen" and make it fit in, you know? But that compartment was full, the next compartment was full, the next compartment was full, and the next compartment...Well, in the last compartment there was one elderly woman. I figured out that if I went in there, that's two, that gives me 50 percent of the conversation. Could I handle it? I had no choice. "Is this place free?"

She nodded; I sat down. She was staring out the window. "Nice day."

She turned and smiled. I worked up another German sentence, a real profound one like, "Will we get there tonight?" She turned and smiled. "You going home?" She turned and smiled. I thought, *Boy, I know more German than she does.* I grew more bold and said, "I'm going to Stuttgart." She turned, smiled. I said, "Where are you going?"

She said, "Rostach." Rostach? Rostach was in Communist Germany, the other side, DDR. Communist Germany.

I said, "Are you a Communist?"

She said, "No. I'm a Christian."

I said, "I'm a Christian."

She looked at me. I said, "I'm from America."

She said, "Yes, I know." We began to talk.

I said, "What's it like to be a Christian in Communist Germany?"

"What's it like to be a Christian in America?" she said. "My grandchildren call America the happy land."

I said, "Well, it's not too happy lately." It was in the late 1960s, and we had assassinations and terrible things. I said, "America's not a happy land now."

She said, "Oh, yes, because in America you don't throw old women away."

I said, "What do you mean?"

She said, "When I got my papers to visit outside Communist zones for one month to visit my grandchildren, I said to the officer, 'What if I don't come back?' And he said, 'Oh, you'll be back, you have family here. But even if you don't, who cares? You're just an old woman.'"

I said, "Well, no, we don't do that in America." She had a music box she'd bought. You twisted it, and as it unwound it played "Silent Night, Holy Night." She twisted it, it began to play, and she sang it in German. She said, "You sing a stanza," which I'm not going to do tonight, but I did on the train. We had a wonderful time.

I had that old sandwich I had bought, and my stomach was growling. I was hungry, but I didn't want to eat my sandwich in front of her. I didn't know what to do. Finally I thought, *I can at least share the sandwich*. Then I ran up against another problem: It was a German sandwich, and the bread was extremely hard. You probably know about German sandwiches. I couldn't get it into two. I'm breaking it over my knee, trying to get the sandwich in two so I can share, and finally when it broke, I pulled a part of it to hand to her. I hadn't noticed, but in the meantime she had peeled an orange and was extending to me half as she received half a sandwich. Half a sandwich, half an orange. We talked of being Christian in Germany and in America. We got to Stuttgart.

"God go with you."

"And God go with you." I could've sworn we had communion on the train. I thought of her tonight. I wonder if she has thought of me. Since I was with her, I have been in 200 churches, I suppose, and the first thing I do when I go to a church is study the menu. I find it's the same in every church. One half sandwich, one half orange; it's the Christian way. I thought of her tonight. In fact, I thought about her so much that I got to thinking how far it is from Springfield, Missouri, to Rostach, Germany. Do you have any idea how far that is, how many hundreds, how many thousands of miles it is? From Springfield to Rostach. Do you know how far it is? I checked the atlas. It's across that table. That's how far it is.

A few years ago in a church in Oklahoma where I was worshiping with my family, I had an afternoon engagement and had to leave quickly. I said goodbye to them after the benediction. In order to get to the parking lot quickly, I cut through the back, through the choir room. I said to one of the women in the choir as she was putting away her robe, "I appreciated very much the anthem this morning."

She said, "I hope so, because that's it."

I said, "What do you mean?"

She said, "That's it. I'm hanging it up." She was putting away her robe.

I said, "Are you retiring?" She'd been in the choir 103 or 104 years; I thought she was retiring.

She said, "No, I'm quitting."

I said, "You're quitting?"

She said, "I'm quitting."

"Oh, you're not quitting."

"I'm quitting."

"Well, why are you quitting?"

She said, "I sat up there in the choir loft this morning and looked around at the other choir members. I looked at the minister and looked at the worship leader. I looked at the ushers and just looked out over the congregation. I said finally to myself what has haunted me for years."

I said, "What's that?"

She said, "Who cares?"

Well, I was in a hurry, I had to make a speech, so I said, "Oh, you'll be all right. Take an aspirin, you've got a headache, all right?" I went to the parking lot, but all the way to my engagement and all the way back I thought of that indictment. I was a member of that church at the time, and she was indicting me and all the members. In fact, if it were true, what she had said was, "This is not a church." If her opinion after longtime membership there, as an active participant in that church, was that the sum gesture of that church was a shrug of the shoulders, then it was not a church.

When I got home that afternoon, I called that lady. I said, "I want to talk to you."

She said, "If you want to."

I said, "I want to." I went over there; we talked, and brusquely we disagreed. I finally asked her, "Well, what would we have to do to show that we cared?"

And this was her definition: She said, "Take me seriously." That was a strange way to put it, especially for her. She was a kind of comic, a sort of stick of peppermint; she was always playing practical jokes. She would pin tails of choir robes together. She would go early and put some big cartoon on the pulpit so that when the minister came out in all his sobriety, he'd look down and be blown out of the water. She was that kind of person, so I said, "You can't be serious! Take you seriously? What are you talking about? You're always joking, laughing."

And she said, "You bought all that? I thought it was rather transparent, myself. I like to be taken seriously."

When I left that lady's house, I said to her, "You're wrong, you're wrong."

She said, "I'm not."

I said, "I get to travel to churches all over the country, and everywhere I go there are people who care for each other. They take care of each other."

She said, "Where?"

I said, "Everywhere I go, there are people who care."

She said, "Really?"

"Yes."

She said, "Name some."

She wants names. May I use your name? May I give her your name?

I recall some years ago being asked to go some distance to a meeting. A fellow going to the same meeting lived near me and said, "You want a ride?"

I said, "Yeah. Save me the gasoline, the tear and wear."

He said, "I'll stop by for you."

When he came by, in the backseat were his wife, whom I had not met, and a daughter. She'd just graduated from college, a very attractive young woman. They were already in the backseat and said, "Sit up there and y'all can talk."

I said, "All right."

They said, "We're not going to the meeting; we're just going shopping."

So we started out on this 200-mile trip. We'd gotten out about twenty-five miles, and his wife, sitting directly behind him, said, "You're going too slow," so he speeded up. Then she said, "You're going to kill us all." He slowed down. She said, "We'll never get there. Are you going to pass here?" So he didn't pass. She said, "Why are you waiting in line?" He started to pass around when she said, "You're going to pass all these cars?" So he got back in line. She said, "Don't you see the yellow line? We're in the wrong lane." Pick, pick, pick, pick, pick. Pretty soon the daughter joined in, and this man was sitting there in silence. I was all embarrassed. What do you do? You don't want to be there. You'd rather be walking. So what do you do? I just sat there kind of stewing. I said to myself, *If this fellow were a man, if he really were a man, he'd pull this car over and leave a couple. Then he and I'd go on to our meeting.*

Well, the farther we traveled, the more I began to say to myself, *Now, if this fellow were a man.* Because I couldn't take it. When we got there, the wife and daughter went shopping. He and I had a few minutes, and he said, "You want some coffee?"

I said, "Fine." We went into a little place, and we sat there staring at the coffee. What do you say? How do you start a conversation? I knew, and he knew, and he knew that I knew. What do you do? I was just staring at my coffee as though it were real interesting coffee.

Finally he said, "Fred, you teach in a seminary?"

I said, "Yeah, yeah."

He said, "I mean, you're into religion and all that?"

"Yeah."

"I mean, you know the Bible and Christianity."

"Yeah. What are you talking about?"

He said, "Well, I just wondered, in your study and in your opinion, what hope do you think there is for a man who has everything in life at age fifty, everything in life he wants, except the one thing he wants the most?"

I used to go home to west Tennessee, where an old high school chum of mine had a restaurant. I called him Buck. Go home for Christmas, "Merry Christmas, Buck," and I'd get a piece of chess pie and cup of coffee free. "Merry Christmas, Buck," I'd say. Every year it was the same.

I went in, "Merry Christmas, Buck."

He said, "Let's go for coffee."

I said, "What's the matter? Isn't this the restaurant?"

He said, "I don't know. Sometimes I wonder."

We went for coffee. We sat there and pretty soon he said, "Did you see the curtain?"

I said, "Buck, I saw the curtain. I always see the curtain."

What he meant by *curtain* is this: They have a number of buildings in that little town; they're called shotgun buildings. They're long buildings and have two entrances, front and back. One's off the street, and one's off the alley, with a curtain and the kitchen in the middle. His restaurant is in one of those. If you're white, you come off the street; if you're black, you come off the alley.

He said, "Did you see the curtain?"

I said, "I saw the curtain."

He said, "The curtain has to come down."

I said, "Good. Bring it down."

He said, "That's easy for you to say. Come in here from out of state and tell me how to run my business."

I said, "Okay, leave it up."

He said, "I can't leave it up."

I said, "Well, then take it down."

"I can't take it down." He's in terrible shape. After a while he said, "If I take that curtain down, I lose a lot of my customers. If I leave that curtain up, I lose my soul."

We had a pastor in my church in west Tennessee years ago that did it. I was only ten, eleven, and twelve during his ministry, but he sure made a believer out of me. I remember one Sunday up on the pulpit there was something with a cloth draped over it, and everything prior to that, the singing, the anthem, and everything, was really just preliminary. Everybody was staring at it. Time for the sermon came, he lifted the corners of the cloth, and there was a skeleton. I learned later he got it from the dentist's office.

As he preached his sermon, he would take a finger and hit the chin of that skeleton. The teeth would click every time he made a point in his sermon. I was sitting there with my mother and saying to myself, *I don't want to go to hell; I really don't want to go to hell.* I remember him describing hell. I can almost remember the phrases: the darkness, and the bottomless pit, and the falling and the screaming, and the hellhounds born every minute, and the bleached bones that wash up on the shore of the lake of fire.

And he said, "Do you know how long that's going to last? Do you have any idea how long you're going to be there? Just imagine," he said, "a granite mountain five thousand feet high. A dove flies by that mountain once every five hundred years and touches the mountain with the tip of his wing. When that dove has worn that mountain down level with the ground…that, in hell, is before breakfast. That's how long it is."

Now, when you're eleven years old…he made the point.

When I started out in the classroom, I would disguise my "I don't know" and try to dazzle my students with a lot of verbal footwork, but I could tell by the way they looked at me that they realized I didn't know. As I got older, more chastened by my own ignorance, I said, "I don't know" more frequently and with less pain. Now, some people, you don't ever expect them to say, "I don't know."

Nettie and I heard, some years ago, the chief of staff at Georgetown University Hospital in Washington, D.C., both publicly and in private at the table, say, "I don't know." A Nobel Prize–winning scientist at Princeton University that a number of us were gathered to hear speak about the frontiers of medicine and science opened the floor for questions. There were questions about cancer, AIDS, and Alzheimer's disease, and to every question, he said, "I don't know."

But even so, you never expect Jesus to say, "I don't know." It's disappointing. In fact, when the scribes sat and copied the scriptures— you know, hand by hand, word by word, faithfully copying it exactly as it was—and they got to Matthew 24:36, when they came to the expression, "Jesus said, 'I don't know,'" they couldn't write it, so they left it out. And we still have copies of those ancient manuscripts in which reverent, God-fearing scribes said, "I can't write those words! I can't stand for Jesus to say, 'I don't know.'"

I went to the Thanksgiving service down at Temple Baptist Wednesday night. I could hardly worship. There was a couple in front of me that talked through the whole service. He and she talked through the whole service. They weren't young people, you know, they were nearly as old as I am. They were punching each other and talking about everybody sitting in the choir. "See that woman up there? We went to school together, that's before we moved away. I never knew she could sing. I don't know what she's doing up there." They went on like that, and just like two mean ducks, picked apart everybody up there. Why did they come? If you're not going to be awake; if you don't enter every room, every relationship, every moment saying, "This could be it," you will miss the coming. Stay alert; stay alert.

You know, I had a thought, not much of a thought, but a thought. Suppose, let's just suppose, that God, who is so full of surprises, were to come among us as a baby—a crying, red-faced Jewish baby, seven pounds, three ounces, kicking arms and legs, with a band around the middle holding the tied cord, a mother attending, and a poor carpenter man standing there looking on. What if God were to do it that way? Do you think you'd miss it? I'm going to stay awake. I wouldn't miss it for the world.

When I was a senior in college, our class, like all senior classes, decided to do some little project on campus and then put up a huge bronze plaque saying, "Gift of the senior class of," and so forth. You know how it goes. We decided to renovate and redecorate an old classroom that was horrible to look at. It needed to be fixed up, so we said, "We'll do that."

We had our committees choosing colors and so forth, and on Saturdays we'd go to work on that room. We scraped paint that was a dark ugly green and peeling off the wall. We scraped green, and it was yellow under that; then we scraped yellow, and it was brown under that; and we scraped brown, and it was green again; and we scraped green—eighty years of paint, layer upon layer.

Finally, when we reached the wood, we noticed how beautiful it was, so we just cleaned off all the paint. And when we saw the wood, the wood as God had created it, it was unbelievably beautiful. The class voted unanimously, "Forget the paint. We'll leave it as it was." We put a finish on it, and the room was delightful to behold. Down to the way God made it, just clean off the crud. Maybe that's what John was saying. I think so. I really think so.

I recall in the 1960's there was what was called the Second Vatican Council of the Roman Catholic Church. Changes were made in the Roman Catholic Church that were the most radical in centuries, so radical in fact that Rome knew that the churches and especially the priests would be upset. So teams of folk were sent to go to the churches, to go to the gatherings of priests all over this country and Europe and talk with them about the changes and try to get them to understand. They anticipated strong negative reactions, and so it was.

Although a Protestant, I was asked to join a Jesuit priest and to go along as one of these teams. Since the changes in the Roman Catholic Church involved more preaching, they thought maybe a Protestant who was in the field of preaching might be helpful to the exercise, and so I went. I learned a great deal. The Jesuit priest, Father Gene Monihan, was a prince of a man, a marvelous man, and I learned so much from him.

I remember our first session. I was just sitting in the front row because I was to take part in the discussion. I had no formal presentation that day. Out onto the platform came Father Monihan, who was barefooted. He had on a pair of little white-washed trousers and a T-shirt, an undershirt, and that's all. He looked out at the priests and said, "I am fifty-four years old. I have spent most of my adult life with my back turned to the congregation as I ministered to the altar. Now my church says, 'Turn around and face the people.' I have spent most of my life hiding among the incense pots and the candles, doing my work as a clergyman, and now the church says, 'Come out and be with the people.' I have spent most of my adult life saying the mass in Latin, and now my church says, 'Speak English, so the people will understand,'" and on and on he went, describing the changes. When he came to the end, he said to the priests that were gathered, "As you can see, I have been stripped of almost everything. All that I have left is God." I sat there in a pool of tears.

How true, not just of Roman Catholics and Protestants, but every human being. In the final analysis, all we have is God. May I make a suggestion? When you get to Bethlehem, as you approach the stable, when you come up to the crib to see the baby, say, "Jesus, here I am, very much like you, just a little child."

I heard last week about a young man, thirty-four years old, who has Guillain Barré syndrome, the unusual kind of paralysis that I had in '92 and '93. He is now in a ventilator in DeKalb Medical Center, the same place I spent six weeks. When I heard the news about his being there, all that came back to me: the smells and the sounds. One of the worst sounds was the nurse coming in at night and pulling up those bars on the sides of the bed, clicking them into place, locking them into place. We called them bars, but for the person lying there, it's not only a sound. It's a prison. I remember one night, the nurse came in and she pulled those into place, click, click. I said, "Why are you doing that? I can't move. I'm not going anywhere." She said, "Oh, we don't want you to roll out of bed." And I said to her, "I wish I could roll out of this bed and roll down the hall and roll out the front door and be free."

Something is getting to John. He has sunk into doubt. He has been plunged into confusion. "Are you he, or shall we look for another?"

I read something recently—I knew this, but I had forgotten about it— that years ago our ancestors used to go out walking, usually on a Sunday afternoon—sometimes alone, sometimes couples, sometimes the whole family—and they called it "going marveling." Marveling. They would look for unusual rocks, unusual wild flowers, shells, four-leafed clovers, marvelous things. They would collect them, bring them back to the house, and show off the marvelous things they had found. Isn't that a delightful thing, to go marveling?

When I read that and was reminded of that, I went marveling myself. You know I live about a mile from here; if you walk down the railroad, it's about a mile. So I left the house and went marveling. About a mile away I came upon a pavilion, and inside I saw a lot of people singing, praying, and reading scripture, sharing their love for each other. They were vowing that they would—they promised to each other, and they promised to God—make every effort, God help them, to reproduce the life of Jesus in this place. And I marveled, how I marveled. And I said to myself, *Look what I have found, right here, in this little building.*

-→=◎ ✛ ◎=←-

G eneral Eisenhower said that in his family they had to read the Bible through every so often, completely, but that he was given permission to skip the genealogy. Well, we're not going to skip the genealogy, because what it is, really, is a walk through the family graveyard of Jesus. It can be awesome. It's not morbid. Some people think of going to a cemetery as morbid, but it doesn't seem that to me.

This summer, our family was at Arlington National Cemetery— nothing morbid and very inspiring. Once in New Haven, Connecticut, I just happened upon the grave of Nathan Hale. "I regret that I have but one life to give for my country." It was an awesome moment, inspiring. Some of you have been to these places. You just can't believe all the feelings that come.

Sometimes it can be embarrassing, because you come across the graves of folk you wish weren't kin. I remember my sister was in pursuit of Ruby, Ruby Craddock. The other Craddocks had come to this country from Wales, but she hadn't come. So my sister, heavy into genealogy, was pursuing Ruby. She told me once, "I found Ruby!"

I said, "Good! What did you find out about Ruby?"

And she said, "You don't want to know." Ruby, instead of coming to America, went to London and opened a brothel. I assured my sister that that was another branch of the family and not to worry about it.

Going to cemeteries can be a strange, mysterious thing. South of Atlanta, there is a cemetery in a small town that still haunts me. There was a very large family, and all the members are buried together in this large plot, except for one. By the inscription on the marker he is a son, and he is buried I would say fifty yards away, all by himself. I just hate all the thoughts that come to my mind. You see, lots of graveyards are mysterious.

I went last week with Fred Dickey from California, who wanted to take me out to Hogback Mountain and see the Dickey graveyard. The Dickey graveyard is an unusual one; it's very old. Though there are many of them, the Dickeys have become famous through one of their members, James Dickey, who wrote *Deliverance* and some other things like that. And Mrs. Dickey was a member of the Taylor family, Zachary Taylor's family. He was president of the United States. All this seemed very important, so I said to Fred Dickey from California, one of the family, "Sure, I'd like to see it." So we went out on a Saturday morning to Hogback Mountain. About forty feet square, with a concrete wall now broken in places, and at the end of it two markers—George Dickey and Hannah Dickey. There are twenty-seven other markers without a name on them, just fieldstones stuck in the ground at different angles, twenty-seven of them. Twenty-nine graves in all; two with names, twenty-seven without. They were slaves. The owners were buried with their slaves? I wish I knew about that. The slave and owner in the same little field. Cemeteries can really be unusual.

So we go with Matthew to the cemetery holding the remains of the family of Jesus.

This is such a dazzling and beautiful story; it still pains me a bit that this story caused me such grief in my early years. When I was eighteen years old, the pastor of the church at home, knowing that I had already indicated a desire to prepare for the ministry, asked me to fill in for him at a little church at Gleason, Tennessee, for a midweek service. I was frightened to death. I prepared what I could, and I said what I could. It wasn't long, it wasn't eloquent, and it wasn't full of substance, but I got through it. Almost. Near the end of my presentation, whatever the subject was, I said something about the visit of the three wise men. No sooner had I said that, than a man in the back of the room, an elderly man, stood up and said, "What gave you an idea that there were three?" Well, I was absolutely dumbfounded and silenced and frightened. I was glad to get out of there and glad to get home. I had serious doubts about going into the ministry. What a painful thing it was, his stopping me in the middle of my sermon and his questioning the three wise men.

I looked it up in the text again, and sure enough, I couldn't find any indication that there were three. I know tradition says three, based on the fact that there were three gifts—gold, frankincense, and myrrh. But in my wiser years I now understand that if there had only been three, they weren't very wise, crossing that desert with all the bandits and marauders behind every sand dune and at every oasis. Not wise men, if only three.

There is a little community in southwest Oklahoma, near the Washita Creek, where the Native American Black Kettle and most of the women and children of his little tribe were massacred by General Custer as he and his troops swept down in the early morning hours. The community is named for the general, Custer City. Nettie and I ministered there about three years; the population was 450 on a good day. There were four churches: a Methodist church, a Baptist church, a Nazarene church, and a Christian church. Each had its share of the population on Wednesday night, Sunday morning, and Sunday evening. Each had a small collection of young people, and the attendance rose and fell according to the weather and whether it was time to harvest the wheat and all of that.

But the most consistent attendance in town was at the little café where all the pickup trucks were parked, and all the men were inside discussing the weather, and the cattle, and the wheat bugs, and the hail, and the wind, and are we going to have a crop. All their wives and sons and daughters were in one of those four churches. The churches had good attendance and poor attendance, but the café had consistently good attendance, better attendance than some of the churches. They were always there. Once in a while they would lose a member there at the café, because their wives finally got to them or their kids, and you'd see them go sheepishly off to one of the churches. But the men at the café still felt strong. "We are still the best, biggest, and strongest group in town." And so they met on Wednesdays and Sundays and every other day, discussing weather and crops—not bad men, but good men, family men, hard-working men.

The patron saint of the group that met at the café was named Frank. Frank was seventy-seven when I met him. He was a good, strong man; a pioneer, a rancher and farmer, and a prospering cattle man too. He was born in a sod house; he had his credentials, and all the men there at the café considered him their patron saint. "Ha! Ol' Frank will never go to church." I met Frank on the street one time. He knew I was a preacher, but it has never been my custom to accost people in the name of Jesus, so I just was shaking hands and visiting with him, but he took the offensive. He was not offensive, but he took the offensive. He said, "I work hard, I take care of my family, and I mind my own business. Far as I'm concerned, everything else is fluff." You see what he told me? "Leave me alone, I'm not a prospect." I didn't bother Frank. That's why I, the entire church, and the whole town were surprised, and the men at the café church were absolutely bumfuzzled when old Frank, seventy-seven years old, presented himself before me one Sunday morning for baptism. I baptized Frank. Some of the talk in the community was, "Frank must be sick. Guess he's scared to meet his maker. They say he's got heart trouble. Going up there and being baptized, well, I never thought ol' Frank would do that, but I guess when you get scared…" All kinds of stories.

But this is the way that Frank told it to me. We were talking the next day after his baptism, and I said, "Uh, Frank, you remember that little saying you used to give me so much: 'I work hard, I take care of my family, and I mind my own business'?"

He said, "Yeah, I remember. I said that a lot."

I said, "You still say that?"

He said, "Yeah."

I said, "Then what's the difference?"

He said, "I didn't know then what my business was." He discovered what his business was—to serve human need. And so I baptized Frank. I raised my hand and I said, "In the presence of those who gather, upon your confession of faith in Jesus Christ, and in obedience to his command, I baptize you in the name of the Father, the Son, the Holy Spirit. Amen."

I remember when we lost our farm when I was a kid. We moved into town to a little four-room house, a small house on a dirt street on the south side of the little town. We had one spigot out in the yard, but no water in the house, no electricity, and the toilet was out back. We were poor as Job's turkey and having a rough time.

My sister was entering high school. She had trouble with her complexion when she was moving into her teens, you know, a pockmarked face and always worrying about it and keeping her head down and combing her hair over part of her face. She was bothered by it, and it was just terrible.

One day in the mail my sister got an invitation from Cullen Lyle to a slumber party. Now you don't know Cullen, but she was the prettiest girl in high school. Her father was a wealthy businessman, and they lived up on Main Street, and my sister got an invitation to her slumber party. And I heard my sister after she was seventy years old speak of the importance of that.

If I can drop a footnote here: If you are poor, and exclude prosperous people because you think they're smart, or if you're prosperous and exclude the poor—you have a right to do that, but it's not church.

I remember hearing President Laney, who was president of Emory University and then ambassador to Korea, talk about his grandfather in Arkansas. His grandfather had so much encouragement around home and in his family that some folks put together the money for him to go to Hendrix College in Conway, Arkansas. He had such a good record at Hendrix that some folks got together and sent him off with a scholarship to Vanderbilt University for graduate school. He met a beautiful young woman, and they married, and he graduated. Then what? You know what he did? He went to northwest Arkansas, and he and his pretty new bride started a school for girls. She did the washing, the cooking, and the cleaning, and he was the principal and the teacher. Now girls, in that day and in northwest Arkansas, weren't even encouraged to go to high school, much less to college, so they started a school for poor girls. Now, he has a graduate degree from Vanderbilt, but he knew what a burden a gift is.

I went to Fifth Avenue Presbyterian Church in New York some years ago to preach in the absence of the minister. They gave their minister thirteen weeks off in the summer. Those places, I think that's a nice idea…write that down. Different ministers filled in. This is a big church; I guess there were a couple of thousand people there that Sunday. Before I went to preach, I got a letter from Steve Kechelino. He sang in the choir, and he was in New York studying opera. His note was this: "Would you be willing to stay after church and have lunch with some of us and talk about the Christian life?" I sent him a note that said I'd be glad to.

So after church, here were these young people in their late teens, twenties, maybe some of them as much as thirty, all of them in New York to try to make it on the stage or in music—Julliard school of music and opera, groups forming rock bands and all—and we went in the kitchen and fixed some soup and salad. I ate with them, and then we moved back into the sanctuary. There were about 250 of them. They were in New York, away from home; they weren't even supposed to be in church! They asked me to stay with them, and we talked about the Christian life. We had a wonderful discussion. I said to them, "I'm really surprised to see you here. You're away from home, and you're trying to make it in New York, and this is the city, and all of that."

During the discussion a young fellow stood up, and after asking him where he was from, I said, "What are you doing in New York?"

He said, "I'm trying to form a rock band."

I said, "Well, what does this mean to you?"

He said, "If you have a gift and forget the giver, all you really have is talent, and talent isn't everything." And he sat down. Wasn't that something? If you forget the giver, all you have left is talent, and talent isn't everything.

Some years ago, in Minneapolis I attended a service of Native Americans. A bunch of us were there at a meeting, and we went to a Native American Christian church. The minister was a Choctaw, a good minister, and the people were lively and interesting. On the table, in addition to the elements and the offering tray, were a blanket draped over the front, an Indian blanket with a beautiful design, and a peace pipe. The blanket, we all sat together on the blanket, and that was a symbol of community and conversation. The peace pipe, you know what that meant. It was beautiful, and it was a great service.

I talked to the minister, the Choctaw, afterward, and he said, "You know, sometimes I think of taking the blanket and the peace pipe away."

I said, "Why? That's very meaningful to you."

And he said, "Yeah, but a lot of whites come, and they're impressed with the peace pipe and the blanket. So they go back to their churches and hang blankets and peace pipes on their altars, just like 'This is so deeply meaningful.' It's *not* meaningful! It's meaningful to *us*!"

Down at the Ray of Hope Christian Church, which is a large, predominantly African American church in Atlanta, when the congregation was being formed, Nettie was on the committee to get the church started. I was there at the service. There were some white people there, but not many. We all ate together. After the service was over, the leader, their minister Cynthia Hale, asked us to form a circle around the building where they were meeting. It had been a Lutheran church building. We formed a circle, and I was standing next to this boy, who looked to be about six or seven, a black child. The minister said, "Take hands, and we'll have prayers around the room," so I took his hand. When I took his hand, he looked up at me and said, "Are you a mean man?"

I said, "No, I'm not a mean man."

When it was over, his father over on the other side of the boy said, "I'm sorry about what he said. It's my fault."

I said, "Well, I wasn't hurt by it. I'm sorry he felt that I might be a mean man."

He said, "It's because you're white. I have suffered so much that, in the afternoon after work, I take it home, and his young ears have picked up the things I've said. So he asked you because you're white, 'Are you mean?'"

It was painful. He was probably six. Your children at school can hear ethnic, ugly things, and you've got to spend half your time clearing that out, because it's wrong. But it's hard to converse across the gulf of race.

I was asked to speak at a big church convention of a major denomination in Las Vegas. Why they had the church assembly in Las Vegas…okay, it was in Las Vegas. I went out of the hotel and asked for a cab to take me out to the convention center where the gathering was being held. I got in and I told him where I was going, and he said, "Is that where all those preachers and folks are gathering?"

I said, "Yeah."

He said, "I want to tell you, don't try to convert me. I'm Roman Catholic; I go to Mass; my wife goes to Mass; our kids go to Mass. We're a Catholic family, we're Christians, so if you want to convert someone, get another cab."

I said, "I just want a ride out to the convention center."

And he said, "I've had four people try to convert me this morning, and I'm tired of it!"

A kid comes to school on Monday morning with a big cast on her leg. What happened? "I was in an accident and broke my leg, and here's my long cast and a crutch." Suddenly, here are all the other kids, and they're signing the cast. This girl didn't know she had so many friends; she's got ninety-seven names on that cast before noon. "Here, let me help you with that crutch," "Here, I'll take your books," "Here, I'll help you to the cafeteria, and I'll get your tray for you," "Here let me do this, here let me do that." Yesterday she didn't have any friends. Now they're just crawling from everywhere.

A child is sick. He has this long sickness that lasts three months. Mommy's holding him and fretting over the feverish child. There are three other children, and they're not getting any attention. "Peanut butter's on the bottom shelf." Pretty soon one of the other children, after about the second week, comes and says, "Mama, my stomach hurts." You know why? She forgot. She didn't have time—no, she forgot that the children who are well need her too. The children that are happy need her too. The children for whom things are going well need her too.

I remember on the farm in west Tennessee—ugly, ugly recollections in my life—I was born and raised and worked among the black people around there. The white people loved the black people as long as they were dependent. They called them "Aunt" and "Uncle." A black woman would clean your house and would take for her pay the leftovers from your evening meal and go home. They were such nice people. That was one generation. Here comes this black woman, the next generation, down the street. "Well, what are you doing?"

She's dressed up. "Well, it's spring break at the university."

"You're at the university?"

"Yeah."

"What are you doing?"

"I'm in law school."

Boy, I don't know what's happening to these blacks nowadays. Do you have trouble with people who are getting along fine, thank you? I don't know if I should say this, but do we pounce on the misfortunes of others to show how sympathetic and caring we are? And we are, and it's right! But there are a lot of folk, and I mean a lot of folk, who seem to be doing just great, who don't even have anybody to share the good news with.

Last fall my wife, Nettie, and I attended a victory party following a University of Georgia football game. We didn't know anybody there except the couple with whom we were in attendance. It was held in a marvelous home in a suburb of Atlanta—Victorian, restored, beautiful, high ceilings, well appointed, and expensive. A lot of people were there, maybe thirty, thirty-five people, mostly in their thirties, forties, and early fifties. They were all dressed up in the kind of clothing that says, "How 'Bout Them Dawgs." It was quite an exciting thing. We emptied the cars, went inside, and put away the coats. The host and hostess put out those little sandwiches and the drink, and then the talk began, introducing each other around to make sure we all knew each other.

There was an attractive woman there, I don't know her name, a little too bejeweled and overdressed to have just come from a ball game, just dripping with success, as was her husband and all the people there, and she stood up in front of all of us while we were getting into the party and said, "I think we ought to sing the Doxology." Before we could even vote on it, she started. She and a few others sang with gusto. Some stood there and counted their shoelaces, some tried to find a place to set their drinks down because you shouldn't hold one during the Doxology. There were a few who hummed along, like I did. I was sort of in between there; I confess to feeling a bit awkward.

When we finished singing the Doxology, this beautiful woman said, mostly to the men, "You can talk all you want about the running of Herschel Walker, but it was Jesus that gave us the victory."

Somebody said, "You really believe that?"

She said, "Of course I do. Jesus said, 'Whatever you ask, ask for in my name,' and he'll give it to you. So I said, 'Jesus, I want us to win more than anything in the world,' and we won. I'm not ashamed to say that it's because of Jesus, because I'm not ashamed of the gospel."

Some of us were beginning to move to other parts of the house. I walked over toward the kitchen; it was kind of awkward. Most of the people were beginning to go silent, and she said, "I'm not ashamed to just say it anywhere, because Jesus told us to shout it from the housetops." I'm already in the kitchen, and I can hear it.

Some of us were standing in the kitchen, trying to get into some of the details and relive the game that had just been played, when the hostess came into the kitchen. There was a silence when she came in, during which one of the men said to me, "Do you think that woman's drunk?" I said, "Well, I don't know. We just moved to Georgia last year." I mean, I was glad that Georgia won, but I was not feverish about it. As the hostess went about refilling her tray with little sandwiches, she said, if I may quote her, "If she doesn't shut her damn mouth, she's going to ruin my party."

Then I said something, and I don't know why I said it. I never say these things. I said to the hostess, "Are *you* a Christian?"

And she said, "Yes, but I don't believe in just shouting it everywhere."

It was our daughter who instructed me in the matter of treating everyone alike. I tried to carry this over into the church. If I may be auto-biographical for a moment, I tried to carry over into the church the policy I had with the children: Treat them alike. Even at Christmas, when buying gifts we kept account of the total. The total for John came to $21.93, and Laura's was only $18, so we rushed out the last night and got a little something to make it the same.

Once Laura, as a small child, said, "Daddy, it's not fair to treat John and me the same." She was not asking for more, but different. I learned about making the mistake here as though I am to be the same in every relationship. It's unnatural, and I was restricted by fear and some advice given by well-meaning people.

❊

I t's not uncommon for people to ask things of me that they would be asking of the pastor. Recently, a woman said to me, "While you're here, are you going to preach on heaven and hell and judgment and stuff?" I said, "Well, I hadn't planned on it. Is that important?" She said, "It is to me and my family." I said, "Well, I hadn't planned to do that." And she said, "Well, I just was hoping that you would."

I didn't pay any more attention to it until later that week when she and, I guess, her husband and several children were leaving the church. A daughter stayed behind. I guess she was maybe fifteen or sixteen, a real pretty girl. I could tell she wanted to ask me something. It's kind of the way it is when a professor preaches—people think they know things the pastor doesn't know, and I nourish the fiction, even though I know it's a fiction. I nourish it the best I can. So everybody was gone, her family was out on the parking lot, and here she stayed, nervous, shifting from one foot to another. Pastor was doing those little janitorial duties that every pastor does regardless of how big the church is. You stick around and flip out the lights and all that. When he was away, she said, "May I ask you a question?" I said, "Yes." Her question was this: "Will I go to hell for not wanting to go to heaven?"

Well, a pretty sixteen-year-old girl asking these ultimate questions kind of blew me away for a moment. In fact, I hadn't thought much about things like that—I should, I suppose. In the rearing of our kids, I didn't use heaven and hell talk for any leverage, though I probably should have. I said, "Why in the world are you asking that?" She said, "Well, my mother's real suspicious. Every time I come in, she grills me: Where you been? Who was with you? What'd you do? Every time I leave the house: Where you going? Who you going with? What are you going to do? When are you going to be home? All the time, very suspicious. The way she gets at me is: If you do this, you won't go to heaven! If you don't do that, you won't go to heaven! All the time: You won't go to heaven! You won't go to heaven!" "What my mother doesn't understand is that I'm not interested in going to heaven." Well, I really was at a loss to answer her because I could not dredge up from my own life the time our son and daughter were at that age. I did not use that kind of talk. I had said to John several times, "You're grounded!" but I didn't mean it in any ultimate sense. But I did get the connection between what the mother had asked me and the daughter's question, "Will I go to hell for not wanting to go to heaven?" You see what the family's about and what the church is supposed to do?

"We want some good churches!" the Chamber of Commerce said. The Chamber of Commerce, wanting to rescue the town and give order and meaning to it, advertised that they'd like to have some good churches come. I don't know if you saw the advertisement. They'd like to have some good churches. I'm sure they did not mean to cast any reflection on the ones they had; they just wanted to have some good ones. What *is* a good church? Some people expect the church to deal with their desperate condition. They expect so much. There are so many people who walk out in the morning to go to work, out of just total wreckage—domestic wreckage, personal, all relationships just shot. Trying to hang on, but still feeling more and more a victim. What's a *good* church supposed to do?

I was in a church not long ago in which the minister came to the point in the service where it said, "Moments of fellowship and sharing concern." He said, "We have our moments now, informal, where anyone can share a concern, anything that's happened in your life." The first person stood up and said, "You probably don't know about our new baby girl. We've named her Judith," then gave the weight and all that. Someone else said, "My aunt, who you knew was ill for so long, she's out of the hospital and doing better." Someone else stood up and said, "My sister graduated from Claremont School of Theology last week." The next person said, "I want you all to know that last night, my grandmother died," and the minister said, "Hey, now that's a good one! Do we have any more like that?"

Now, I'm sure he didn't mean to say that, but that's what he said. As if he meant to say, "Let's get all this good news out of here, and have some more of the stuff like that!" Now, I'm telling you the truth, there are places I go where weakness and things like that almost get to the point of being celebrated, so much that if you're not crippled or at least don't have a pretty good limp, you're not in.

I remember Joachim Jeremias, the late grand professor of New Testament at the University of Göttingen in Germany, whose parents were missionaries in Israel. As he said, "Back then, we said, 'Palestine.'" He went home, of course, in the terrible late 30s, and then there was the war, the Holocaust, the killing of the Jews. He said, "When the war was over, I had to return to the place where I had grown up to see if any of the Jewish people would speak to me, would care for me, would love me after six million of their brothers and sisters had been killed by my brothers and sisters."

"I went back to that land, I went frightened to every door, knocking. No one was there. I didn't know anybody. I didn't know anybody. I went to one house, the door opened, and there was a man I knew, a friend of my father's. He recognized me immediately and said, 'Come in.' When I went in, he said, 'We are now observing the Feast of Booths, and we have our little brush arbor out in the back. Won't you come out with us?' I went out in the back with them where they had the brush arbor with the pomegranates hanging down, and they were celebrating the tent life, the life of the tent in the wilderness."

Jeremias said, "When I went in the doorway of their brush arbor, there was a little piece of paper clipped to one side of the door, and the other side of the door. It said one word in Hebrew. I asked my host, 'What is that?' And he said, 'It's a summary of the 139th Psalm.' 'Well, what does it mean?' 'Well, this word is "from God," this word is "to God," and in between, a tent.'" For no human institution, nor any reaction against any institution in an attempt to gain freedom, can possibly hinder the free flow of the grace of God; and all my life I waken each morning with the possibility of being surprised, not only in my own life, but in the life of someone I had not even noticed. God is working now, and so am I.

I recall when I heard the news, the disturbing news about Catherine. When I was a fourth grader, we called her Miss Catherine. Boy, she was beautiful, intelligent, gave a lot of attention to all of us, helped us with arithmetic and everything. All the boys in our class had a crush on her. So it was absolutely devastating when I heard about her. In fact, I didn't believe it. It was all over town, and I was the only one, I simply refused to believe it. The word was that Miss Catherine had had her ears pierced. Well, it couldn't be true, because we knew in that little village in west Tennessee what it meant when a woman had her ears pierced. If there was anything revelatory of character, it was having your ears pierced. She had her ears pierced, they said. My older sister Frieda said, "Catherine had her ears pierced." I said, "She did not!" You see, that meant she was a wanton woman. I just couldn't believe that my teacher had her ears pierced. It hurts me now to think about it. She had her ears pierced! To have her ears pierced meant that we all knew what kind of person she really was—we knew what she did when she went to town; we knew what kind of entries she put in her diary; we knew what she slept in, if anything. That's rough when you're in the fourth grade.

I was going to see a widely publicized painting of Christ that was on tour. There was a long line. I went into this booth, and there was the painting. I suppose it was five feet tall; it's probably life-sized! Jesus was about five feet tall. In this painting was this grotesque, ugly, ugly person. I had always gone to Sunday school in a room that had Solomon's head of Christ—I knew how pretty he was. And here was this grotesque creature. Everybody was pouncing on the painting. "Why in the world?" And someone said, "Haven't you read?" "Haven't we read what?" "He had no comeliness or beauty that we should desire him. He is the one from whom people hide their face. From him they turn away, a man acquainted with sorrow, rejected, despised. Didn't you know?" That's rough.

When you have recently given your life to Christ, and are beginning to hear the first stirrings that soon will be the thundering call to ministry, that is super-intense seriousness. And then you are invited to a party where you can already hear the music. Strange enough, as I approached the door, the music was "Just a Closer Walk With Thee," and I thought, *Boy, this is going to be really something. Just a closer walk with thee.* I opened the door, and everybody was dancing, cheek to cheek. Just a closer walk with thee. Grant it Jesus if you please, and here were people dancing?! Absolutely devastating.

I recall waiting in the airport at Portland, Oregon, for a plane back to Atlanta and visiting in a casual way with a couple. They were in their seventies, I guess, and had been to Hawaii. They were brown as gingerbread, and he still had the lei around his neck, a big straw hat, and gifts for all the grandchildren. He fell over onto the floor, and the paramedics were there, I suppose, in two minutes. Just like that they were there, but there was nothing they could do. When he fell, he broke his glasses. I was visiting with her afterward, and this was her part of the conversation: "And I didn't bring another pair of glasses," she said. "He had another pair and he put them out and told me, 'Remember to take another pair of glasses,' and I forgot. I left those glasses…That's the only pair of glasses he had. Now what are we going…" And she talked about those glasses while he lay there dead. She was in shock, which is a providential way of protecting us from death until we are able to make sense out of the nonsensical. Now, I don't mean disturbing in the sense of sudden shock; I mean disturbing in the sense of the profundity of its importance. What if something happens to you that forces you to return to the quarry from which you were mined and rethink values, loyalties, commitments, ideas? It can happen. It happened to the disciples.

Just think of what a refrain will do—consider some examples. Remember the funeral oration of Marc Antony at the grave of Julius Caesar in Shakespeare's play? "Friends, Romans, countrymen,…I come to bury Caesar, not to praise him. The evil that men do lives after them, the good is oft interred with their bones…The noble Brutus hath told you Caesar was ambitious;…and Brutus is an honorable man." He talks awhile, then "And Brutus is an honorable man," then he talks some more, and then, "And Brutus is an honorable man." After about five or six of "And Brutus is an honorable man," the crowd is screaming. They hate that phrase "And Brutus is an honorable man" because now they hate Brutus, and they are screaming, "Kill!" Now what did it? A refrain; for the task of the refrain is to move the burden of the speech away from the speaker onto the listener so that the listener is in on it. An oral presentation has to travel kind of light, and it doesn't have very long to achieve its task of getting the group to say, "That's what we believe." A refrain can do it.

Take the saloon song, the old saloon song "Frankie and Johnny"; do you know "Frankie and Johnny"? Shame on you if you know this song, but I will make an allusion and quotations. "Frankie and Johnny" was originally "Frankie and Albert," but it didn't have a ring to it, so it was changed to "Frankie and Johnny." Now I want you to listen to a refrain— I'll go through a part of it. Listen to the refrain and listen to the function of the refrain. "Frankie, she was a good woman, and Johnny, he was her man. And every silver dollar that Frankie made went straight into Johnny's hand. He was her man, but he done her wrong." Uh-oh. See? Something's going to happen, you just don't know what it is yet. "Frankie and Johnny went walking, Johnny wore a new linen suit. 'Cost me a hundred,' said Frankie, 'but don't my Johnny look cute?' He was her man, but he done her wrong. Frankie went down to the corner, and she ordered a thimble of gin. She said to the fat bartender, 'Has my lovin' Johnny been in?' He was her man, but he done her wrong. 'Ain't gonna tell you no story, ain't gonna tell you no lie. Johnny was here about an hour ago with a floozy named Nellie Bly.' He was her man, but he done her wrong." Uh-oh, it's coming now.

Well, I'm not going to go through the whole thing—it's in the Methodist Hymnal, so you can find the words. But that refrain creates anticipation; it builds to the act itself. Think of the refrain preaching of Martin Luther King, Jr. "I have a dream," over and over and over until everybody in this country says it. He said in that sermon in Washington, "Let freedom ring," and he described the distances. "Let freedom ring," he said five times. "Let freedom ring," and the whole country says it—"I have a dream—I have a dream!" In a matter of a few minutes, the speech of one man to a large crowd became the speech of a large crowd to the world. And how is it done? By refrain. Martin Luther King, Jr., knew the tune as well as the words to a sermon. And Luke does the same thing.

I began my ministry in Appalachia. The majority of the congregation I served could not read and write. I appointed myself, while I was there, economic adviser. These people lived in what the government called a "pocket of poverty." Very small incomes. They got those little checks, those measly little checks, and invariably spent part of it buying flowers, or whatnots to hang on the wall, or some beads, or baubles of some sort. I would argue with those people. I'd say, "Look, why should roses and petunias cover the ground when you could plant potatoes and onions and feed your kids?" So impractical. So impractical, the little trinkets on the wall, and those beads, and there's a man with a little thing hanging down from his bibbed overalls on his chain. It cost him three dollars—it's nothing, it's a trinket.

One day I was fussing at Miss Glover. She didn't have the money, and there she was with some little something; you couldn't eat it, you couldn't play with it, you couldn't do anything but look at it. And I said, "Miss Glover, it's a waste. You can't afford that!" She looked at me and said, "Brother Craddock, everybody's got to have some pretties." Now you would say it another way, but if your understanding of human nature is the being who traces the course of the stars, thinks the thoughts of God after God, understands the Pleiades, sings, dances, writes poetry and music, then she's right for you too. Everybody's got to have some pretties. Once in a while, pretty rare I must admit, I would have a phrase or a line in one of my sermons, and I noticed the people repeating them. I'd go down to the store, and somebody would say that line from my sermon. And in conversation, maybe months later, somebody would be saying that line. Why? Because that was the one true thing that I said? It wasn't because it was true. It was the way it sounded. It *was* true, but it was the way it sounded.

I remember what Miss Glover said: "Everybody's got to have some pretties." That's not decoration; that's not embroidery; that is a fundamental human need. T. S. Eliot said of poetry, "Poetry is not simply the assertion of something being true, but the making of that truth more real for all of us."

About twelve or fifteen years ago, the Academy of Religion and the Society of Biblical Literature were having an anniversary meeting in Los Angeles. It was a thrilling occasion, a big gathering, perhaps three thousand scholars from around the world, people whose books you'd read, there they were. Seminars and study groups and special meetings and special projects, and the papers were just extraordinary; minute, of course, but extraordinary; strange and removed, but very, very good. We ran from paper to paper and banquet to banquet and conversation to conversation. In the course of one of those hasty journeys in the large hotel where we were, I encountered a woman, frantic fear and high anxiety on her face. Under her arm she clutched a black zippered Bible, and she said, "Are you attending this meeting of Bible teachers?" I said, "Yes." She said, "Is it open to anybody?" and I said, "Well, there are open sessions." She said, "Well, can I come in?" I said, "What's your interest?" She said, "I have wasted my life—I would like to be a Christian." There wasn't anything on the program for her! I didn't dare send her in to Wittgenstein and all that. What was I going to do with this woman? I steered her off to one side, to a refreshment stand, and for over an hour we talked. We talked about being a Christian. Before I left, I marked her Bible for her, some places where she could read upon her return home.

I do not say that in criticism of that meeting. There are no apologies to be made for that meeting, and there is no criticism of that meeting. That meeting was not designed for her, and it would be as stupid to criticize that meeting as it would be to criticize a medical researcher for not seeing patients. But if nobody would have spoken to her, if nobody would have answered her questions, there would be no reason for the American Academy of Religion. There would be no reason for the Society of Biblical Literature.

Scott Momaday teaches literature at the University of California. He was told that his grandmother, the most important woman in his life as a child, was dying, so he dismissed himself from his class and the school and caught a plane, not to the reservation in southern Oklahoma where she lived, but to Montana. There he caught a bus. You see, the Kiowa tribe, of which he was a member, started in the Yellowstone River. That's what his grandmother had said. She said, "Scott, the reason we're such a small tribe is that we came through a hollow log out of the Yellowstone River. Not many of us had gotten through, and one of the squaws, pregnant, got stuck in the log. That's why there's just not many of us." And he remembered her as he rode the bus. Oh, they came through Kansas: "Scott, we didn't just fight the white man, we fought other tribes too. There weren't many buffalo, and the winters were cold. Oh, the blizzards of Kansas…"

He rode the bus, and he remembered. When he got to Oklahoma, to the reservation, to the cemetery, to the gravesite, he probably was the only one at the funeral. You see, you can't take a plane to a funeral. It takes a lot of looking to prepare a sermon.

Fifty years ago in Germany there was that famous debate back and forth between Barth and Brunner over what was called the "point of contact." The question was: What is the point of contact of the gospel upon the ear of an unbeliever? Professor Barth said, "There is no point of contact. The image of God has been totally erased." He said to his students, "Don't ever prepare an introduction to your sermon. What are you trying to do, get them interested? There's nothing there to get interested. Don't get involved in the idolatry of homiletics, trying to be interesting. Just present the gospel. God prepares the ear; God gives the message. Trust totally in God for all of it, and that's it."

And Mr. Brunner said, "No, no, no, no. There is something to the way you craft the sermon. There's many a preacher who will, on account of what is said, go to heaven, but on account of how it is said, go to hell." We have responsibility because there is some capacity in the listener to hear the gospel.

I don't know what's big and what's small. I was in the depot; it was really an airport in Buffalo, New York, and there was a small boy hawking papers. He left a stack of them and carried some of them under his arm, selling papers. A man, a well-dressed man, graying at the temples, saw the boy turn his back on the little stack that was left, and he picked up one, leaving no quarter. Under his arm it went, and he walked away. "Ah—

twenty-five cents. Don't make a big deal. Here, here's five dollars, don't make a big deal out of it." Twenty-five cents. How small. I followed this fellow in the cafeteria line. He was awfully slow, just poking along, so I got to watching his tray as well as mine. We came to those little pats of butter—what are they, a nickel? He took one, lifted a saucer, and put it under there. And when he went by the cashier, he didn't pay. That's only a nickel—I mean, come on, now—let's get with the big stuff, it is only a nickel. In the courtroom it's a nickel, but in character, it is a felony of the grossest proportions. For if a man will steal a quarter from a child, if a well-dressed man will sneak under the saucer a nickel, we're dealing with a criminal.

I don't know what's big and what's small.

I was invited last year, in mid-October, to the University of Winnipeg in Canada to give two lectures, one Friday night and one Saturday morning. I went. I gave the one on Friday night. As we left the lecture hall, it was beginning to spit a little snow. I was surprised, and my host was surprised because he had written, "It's too early for the cold weather, but you might bring a little windbreaker, a little light jacket." The next morning when I got up, two or three feet of snow pressed against the door. The phone rang, and my host said, "We're all surprised by this. In fact, I can't come and get you to take you to any breakfast, the lecture this morning has been cancelled, and the airport is closed. If you can make your way down the block and around the corner, there is a little depot, a bus depot, and it has a café. I'm sorry." I said, "I'll get around." I put on that little light jacket; it was nothing. I got my little cap and put it on; it didn't even help me in the room. I went into the bathroom and unrolled long sheets of toilet paper and made a nest in the cap so that it would protect my head against that icy wind.

I went outside, shivering. The wind was cold, the snow was deep. I slid and bumped and finally made it around the corner into the bus station. Every stranded traveler in western Canada was in there, strangers to each other and to me, pressing and pushing and loud. I finally found a place to sit, and after a lengthy time a man in a greasy apron came over and said, "What'll you have?" I said, "May I see a menu?" He said, "What do you want a menu for? We have soup." I said, "What kinds of soup do you have?" And he said, "Soup. You want some soup?" I said, "That was what I was going to order—soup." He brought the soup, and I put the spoon to it—Yuck! It was the awfulest. It was kind of gray looking; it was so bad I couldn't eat it, but I sat there and put my hands about it. It was warm, and so I sat there with my head down, my head wrapped in toilet paper, bemoaning and beweeping my outcast state with the horrible soup. But it was warm, so I clutched it and stayed bent over my soup stove.

The door opened again. The wind was icy, and somebody yelled, "Close the door!" In came this woman clutching her little coat. She found a place, not far from me. The greasy apron came, "What do you want?" She said, "Glass of water." He brought a glass of water, took out his tablet, and said, "Now what'll you have?" She said, "Just the water." He said, "You have to order, lady." "Well, I just want a glass of water." "Look, I have customers that pay—what do you think this is, a church or something? Now what do you want?" She said, "Just a glass of water and some time to get warm." "Look, there are people that are paying here. If you're not going to order, you've got to leave!" And he got real loud about it. So she got up to leave and, almost as if rehearsed, everybody in that little café stood up and started toward the door. I got up and said, "I'm voting for something here; I don't know what it is." And the man in the greasy apron said, "All right, all right, all right, she can stay." Everybody sat down, and he brought her a bowl of soup.

I said to the person sitting there by me, I said, "Who is she?" He said, "I never saw her before." The place grew quiet, but I heard the sipping of that awful soup. I said, "I'm going to try that again." I put my spoon to the soup—you know, it was not bad soup. Everybody was eating this soup. I started eating the soup, and it was pretty good soup. I have no idea what kind of soup it was. I don't know what was in it, but I do recall when I was eating it, it tasted a little bit like bread and wine. Just a little like bread and wine.

Not too long ago, I returned to Oklahoma to make a speech at a church where I had taught for years. On the plane going into Oklahoma City, three seats across from me, there was a man and his wife, a young couple. I struck up a conversation. I could tell they'd been on a holiday, that they'd been on vacation, because of what they were wearing— some people always wear their vacation home with them. I could not only tell they'd been on vacation, but where they'd been. I said, "You been on vacation?" They said, "Yeah." "You been to Europe?" She said, "Yes!" I said, "What countries did you visit?" He said, "All them little countries crouched up together, where you can't tell when you're in one and out of the other." I knew then that it was her trip, not his, so I asked her, "What was your favorite place?" She said, "Oh, my favorite place was the Alps. Oh, it just took my breath away. I could've spent forever there. We took pictures, but I'm sure they...it's just unbelievable beauty."

The plane lowered; the no smoking and fasten seat belt signs came on. As the plane dipped down toward Oklahoma City airport, she rummaged around through a bag, pulled out a camera, pressed it against the window, and started clicking. I said, "Pardon me, you've been in the Alps and you're taking pictures of Oklahoma?" She looked at me with this level gaze and said, "But this is home."

Sir Walter Scott said: "Breathes there the man with soul so dead / who never to himself hath said, / 'This is my own, my native land.' / Whose heart hath n'er within him burned, / as home, his footsteps he has turned / from wandering on a foreign strand."

I am talking about the word *place*. The daughter said, as she prepared to go back to San Francisco, "Now mother, get your things together. You're going home with us." And the mother said, "No." The daughter said, "Well, now that dad is dead, there's nothing holding you here. We've all moved away, and I don't want you staying here by yourself." "I'm not by myself." "Mother, I don't want to hear anything about it. Get your stuff together, we'll arrange the furniture later, but you're coming home." "No, no, no. I'll stay here. I have my church, and I have my friends, and I have my memories, and this is my place."

Place. The children ran all through this new little house, a bath and five rooms, built by volunteers with Habitat for Humanity. That woman and those three little girls stood there, that woman's eyes brimming with tears, and the children running into each room and back, then pulling at her skirt, "Mama, is this our place? Mama, is this our place?" Off they'd run and back, and she'd say, "Yes. Yes. Yes. Yes." Look at their eyes, really look at their eyes. I'm talking about the word *place*.

I've been trying to trout fish in North Georgia, but I don't know how. I hang up in the trees, and they tell me, "There are no fish in the trees." I was coming out of Cartecay Creek after another unsuccessful day, but I'd gotten wet, and the hook was wet, and I was making progress. There was a man and a woman driving a car down by the bank, then they turned it alongside the creek. They got out as I got out of the creek, and I said, "Going to fish?" He said, "No." They opened the trunk and got out a couple of those little flexi-chairs, folding chairs. I said, "Oh, you going to have a picnic?" He said, "No." Then they put the chairs out in front of the car and sat there. Well, I was ready to go, but couldn't stand it, of course, so I said, "What're you doing?" He said, "I'm a minister in the United Methodist Church. I'm going to retire in two years. We've lived over forty years in the churches' houses, so I bought an acre here along the creek, and we're going to have a place of our own." I'm talking about *place*. You have to have that word to understand the Bible.

I remember asking Rabbi Silberman at Vanderbilt once, years ago— he never used the word *God*—before class, I said, "What is your favorite expression for the almighty, for God?" And he looked at me quickly without hesitation and said, "Of all the names, my favorite is one of the oldest— 'the place.'" God is the place.

Since I've been at Candler, I heard about a young man in his early twenties dying of that horrible, horrible, frightening, terrible AIDS in a hospital in Atlanta. He had no church connection, but someone said he had relatives who had been in the church, so they called a minister of that church, and the minister went to the hospital. The young man was almost dead, just gasping there, and the minister came to the hospital, stood out in the hall, and asked them to open the door. When they opened the door, he yelled in a prayer. Another minister there in south Atlanta, down around Forest Park, heard about it and rushed to the hospital, hoping that he was still alive. She got to the hospital, went into the room, went over by the bed, and pulled a chair by the bed. This minister lifted his head and cradled it in her arm. She sang. She quoted scripture. She prayed. She sang. She quoted scripture. She prayed. And he died. Some of the seminarians said, "Weren't you scared? He had AIDS!" She said, "Of course I was scared. I bet you I bathed sixty times." "Well then, why did you do it?" And she said, "I just imagined if Jesus had gotten the call, what he would've done. I had to go."

I suppose you could say that my goal, my chief ambition in the world, is not just to be a good minister, but to be a Christian minister.

Some friends of ours had a son graduating from high school, so we all went together to the commencement. The commencement speaker used an open door as the governing image of the talk. "Young people," he said, "you stand before an open door." It was a good speech, better than we usually give or hear at commencements, about launching out on the sea of life, standing at the crossroads, having your foot on the first rung of the ladder of success, and those things. It was a good speech; "You stand before an open door. Pass through that door to economic security, higher education, a fulfilled life, and happiness." Only one heavy part of the message at all, and that was in my mind. As I looked at the young people and knew some of their families—or lack of family, as the case was—I knew that for a few in that class, the door was not open. They would not go through to fulfillment, and happiness, and higher education, and economic security. They might crash at the door and get through it, but for them it was, at least temporarily, closed. It was a bit depressing to me through that speech—it had a lilt and lightheartedness to it—but it was a bit depressing to think about it. In fact, the only thing more depressing for me to think about, other than a door being closed, is the closing of the door behind you. You're in and can't get out; to hear the clang of the iron door and know that there's no exit; to be trapped there; to say, "I wanted in, but now I want out."

I was present at only one exiting service in my life. And we didn't know, the congregation and the minister didn't know what was happening until it happened. We had no ritual, no bulletin, no order of service for anybody to un-join the church. She was twenty-eight or twenty-nine years old, and I knew her. In fact, she had been in my class once when I taught at the university. She was a bright woman, she'd been very active in our church, and at the close of the service there was a hymn of invitation to discipleship, and she came down the aisle. We always expect somebody is joining, somebody's moving their membership to our congregation, or somebody's rededicating a life. She was a member, she lived there, she must be coming to rededicate her life; but she'd been so busy and active, why would she do that? Must be emotion; she's overcome with emotion. We were all ready to gather around her, and she asked the minister if she could speak to the congregation. He thought she wanted to say a word of dedication, and he said, "Sure." She turned around and said, "I'm turning it in." She said, "I want you to know it's not you people and it's not this church. It is Christianity. I have tried it. I have made every sincere effort, but I want you to know that with the same sincerity I joined here four years ago, I wish now to have my name removed from the rolls of those who are called 'Christian.'" And she left; the minister standing there fumbling with his bulletin, the rest of us standing around, we didn't know what to do. You don't do the usual thing—"Congratulations!" and all that. There's just no exit, is there, really?

Like the priest in Atlanta—did you read about that? This marvelous young priest gathered up kids from the dark, southwest side of Atlanta, where the houses and the life are just a grind. He got the money, he got a bus, and he picked up those children from poverty and took them to see the pretty things. They went to St. Philip's Cathedral; they went to the High Museum of Art; they went to the Eastern Orthodox Church, which is just a poem of light and color, unbelievable. Those kids spent a whole day of "Ooh" and "Ahh," and they had burgers on top of burgers, and they laughed, and they had a good time. It was getting late, and he said, "Kids, we've got to go," and they got on the bus and went back down there. A thirteen-year-old boy in the group set fire that evening to his own house and the two next to it. But why? "I didn't know until today how ugly they were." That's not what the priest had in mind. If your best effort to love and care and help goes boomerang, where's the exit?

That couple over in Illinois, bless their hearts, with kids in junior high, playing junior high basketball. Their son is kind of awkward and stumbly, but he's, you know, junior high. But one of his classmates was tall and straight, a high scorer on the team. When they beat the other team, there were great cheers and banners and balloons and more hot dogs, and people shouted, "Let's go get something." It had begun to rain, and as they were leaving the gym, they saw this tall topscorer leaving the gym. "You want a ride?" He got in, and they took him by his house, anticipating that there would be celebration and joy, quick calls to grandmother telling her what had happened, and everything. But the house was dark, and nobody was there. "Your folks home?" "No." "Where are they?" "I don't know." They didn't even know he played basketball. "Well, you want to go with us?" "No, I'll just stay here." That couple started thinking, *You know, there may be other kids like that. There may be other kids like that.*

So they started a little program in cooperation with the school— afternoon get-togethers, tutoring for those who were falling behind, some good times on Saturdays, a nice program. Then the rumors started; the rumors started. "Yeah, it looks like they're helping. But you know all that stuff about child abuse and sex abuse we've been reading about? I'll bet you. Yeah, I'll bet you." Not a teacher, not a one of the kids, not any parents said anything like that at all, but somebody can't stand it because somebody else is doing what's right. Now the young couple says, "We can't afford a lawsuit. We just can't fight this rumor, we can't keep…" In other words, they're saying, "Where's the exit?" This is not what they had in mind.

Some folks moved in down the street from us, four little girls, a little boy, and a mother, but we didn't see a man. They seemed to be, from the belongings that were moved into the house, very poor. Nettie went down there, and there was a girl, still small. Nettie said, "They could wear those dresses of Laura's." She had made dresses for our daughter, and they were hanging upstairs. I don't know why we kept them, but—you know—kids rapidly outgrow clothes. They were pretty dresses, just like new. She took seven of them down there. "Here, I believe these'll fit." "Oh yeah, they'll fit." She left them, feeling good about herself. Later she went down there to see how they were doing, and there was a bluetick hound lying on the porch, and three or four of those dresses were a bed for that hound. She came back, and I won't quote what she said, but, why should you try to help anybody?

You remember Charles Dickens commenting once about being in a gathering of divines in a very ecclesiastical setting, and the meeting extended itself a long, long time, droning away on unimportant subjects treated without feeling. Mr. Dickens interrupted the proceedings by saying, "I have a suggestion. Why don't we move to a table, and sit around the table and hold hands, and see if we can make contact with the living."

We've all been to those meetings.

Life is so tenacious and strong. I learned this first when I killed a snake as a boy. I was chopping cotton, that means with a hoe, under the sun, getting the weeds out of the cotton field. I was about seven years old. So I was chopping cotton when I saw a snake coiled before me. I began to chop the snake. I went to tell my father, and he lectured me about killing snakes indiscriminately, but a snake is a snake—it still is, pretty much, a snake. He told me about all the benefits of snakes, and how they kept down the rodents and all, and that I shouldn't do that, and had I already done it. I said, "Yes, I killed him." I went back, and the snake was still moving, the tail was. I went back and said, "I don't think I killed him," and he came over and said, "But he will die." I said, "Well, why doesn't he hurry up and die?" He said, "Oh, snakes never die until sundown." Did you know that? If a turtle snaps you, it won't let loose until it thunders. And if you kill a snake, it will not die until sundown. He said, "Now hang the snake on the fence, and it will die at sundown."

I, without enthusiasm, finished the day of work, always looking over toward the fence, seeing just a little wiggle of the end of the tail. And my last picture at the close of that day was the moving of that snake's tail, and I saw something of the mystery of life and how tenacious and tough it is.

I went to the dedication service of a beautiful building at the University of Oklahoma. It had a tall tower, great facilities, all kinds of marvelous things. I was there for the dedication. And the young man, the campus minister, had a very brief prayer: "Lord, burn down this building and scatter these people for the sake of the gospel."

One summer I was teaching at Princeton. In the refectory, I found a place at a table. There was a young woman there. "You a student?" "Yes, I'm a graduate student." "In what field?" "Theology." "Oh, really?" "Yes." We talked more. She was a Roman Catholic nun—she had not been one for long. She said, "I was a buyer for Macy's in New York. I had a nice apartment, and everything was just really going my way." She said, "In fact, I was engaged to be married. About two months before the wedding, I had prayed, I had thought, I had prayed, I had thought, I called him. He came over, and I gave him the ring. He didn't understand, but he took the ring and he left. Some time later, I was on the subway in New York. I was wearing my nun's habit, and all the seats were taken. I was standing, holding the strap when I suddenly realized, facing me, holding the strap, right in front of me, was he. I said, 'Hello.' He said, 'Hello.'" She said, "We both cried and said goodbye again."

I said, "Does it still hurt?" And she said, "Very much." Then why did she do it? She did it because not everybody lives by the principle "If it feels good, do it."

When we were in Oklahoma, in Kingfisher, a little town near where we lived, they published a paper just about every week. That little town publisher had a weekly paper. One of the articles in it—and our only reason for reading the paper—was an article by an Arapahoe Indian woman. She called herself, in English, Molly Shepherd. Every week there was an article by Molly Shepherd. We read it because, in her delightfully broken English, she told of tribal customs, of songs, and of funerals, and giveaways, and prizes for those who came the farthest to the funeral, and tossing things in a blanket, and giving away everything that the deceased owned. It was interesting; it was educational, the Arapahoe Indians, the Cheyenne Indian customs. We enjoyed it very much. In her own broken

English way, she had a gift of words, and it was sometimes almost poetic and flowing the way she talked.

One article, however, was very brief. I'll never forget it. It was the afternoon paper on Friday following the death of President Kennedy. In that article, she said, "Molly has no words for you today. Molly has nothing to write today. Molly has no words today. Molly goes through the house all day saying, 'Oh…'" Now what is that? Molly's "Oh…" is translated, and she has joined, not disjoined, the travail of the world.

I recall as a youngster having to go get the little red mule we used to plow. We had a little truck garden—tomatoes and cabbage and peas— and we plowed that truck garden farm with a red mule. We never could agree on a name, so we just called it "the red mule." The red mule got out. Our fences were poor, and the red mule would get out. I'd come home from school: "Go get the red mule."

Finding the red mule almost invariably involved going up over a hill and across the back woods where there was the family cemetery. Graves in there dated from the 1700s. It was an old cemetery, with wind whistling in the pines, the carpet beneath making it so silent it was frightening. I would make noises and scuff my feet and whistle and do anything to break up the silence of the place. I hated that mule taking me through that frightening cemetery in the late hours of the day, sometimes almost dark, always behind that graveyard.

When I went for the mule, I said, "Do I have to go through the graveyard?" She said, "There's no other way. Now when you go through the graveyard, make sure you don't step on graves. Graves are sacred ground, and don't step on the graves." These graves, 1791, the ground was level, the little markers leaning over, and the carpet of needles. Where was the grave? I remember how ridiculous I must've looked tiptoeing and taking long steps and then short steps trying to avoid what I did not know—but maybe this is sacred. I went home frustrated with that mule and I said, "Mama, I can't tell what part is sacred." And she said, "Well, I know, it looks the same. But if you'll just treat it all as sacred, you'll never miss."

You treat it *all* as sacred, but that's just the way she was.

It reminds me of the time in the parish in mid-Tennessee. On a rainy day, I would go over to the church, to my study, and I would say to myself, "It's too bad it's raining. If it weren't raining, I would go to the nursing home, and go to the hospital, maybe call on a few of the parishioners. But since it's raining, I'll just kick back with a good book." I'd pull a good book off the shelf, get in a comfortable chair, and lean back. And just as I did, I saw out the window, through the rain, those two Mormon missionaries. I said, "Why don't you guys give me a break? It's raining!" And their zeal ruined my day.

When we were in Oklahoma, an artist of modest reputation painted a portrait of Jesus of Nazareth. Some of us who were in the field of religion were asked to look at it in an early showing. I was absolutely shocked at first. The colors used were all very dark: purples and blacks and grays. The figure was strange and very homely—ugly with a misshapen face. On a little easel next to the painting, the artist had placed what was a justification for this painting. It was based on the prophecy of Isaiah 53: "He had no beauty or comeliness that any should desire him. He was one from whom people turned their face. A man of sorrow, acquainted with grief."

The church in Oklahoma was scandalized, as it was wherever the painting went, until finally someone, I suppose, put it in File 13. I never heard of it again.

When you're raised from the dead, you're different. When you're raised from the dead, you don't look the same, you don't act the same, and you don't sound the same. Now, if they were using words, if they were writers, they could've just written, "He is risen from the dead/ he has triumphed over death/he lives forever/he is seated at the right hand of God." Words can do that. But if you only have paint and brush, how are you going to do it? How do you paint a resurrection "glow"?

That's what was puzzling to me when I was baptized just a couple of weeks short of my fourteenth birthday. The passage I read to you this morning was used by the minister who baptized me: "Now you have been raised with Christ, you have died and now you have been raised with Christ. Set your mind on things that are above." As I walked home with my wet clothes wrapped in a wet towel under my arm, I tried to think what that meant. You know, after you've been raised from the dead, you don't look the same, sound the same, talk the same, do the same. But what do you do? How do you talk? What do you sound like?

I went to school Monday morning thinking, *Is anybody going to know that I've been raised? Should I dress up a little better from what I've been dressing? It wouldn't hurt. Do I talk another way? Do I throw in a verse of scripture now and then? What do I do at ball practice? Are they going to say, "Well, looks like he's been raised from the dead."* How do you talk? How do you walk? How do you relate?

My brothers and I used to mow the cemetery lots at Rose Hill cemetery in Humboldt, Tennessee. It was a way of helping support the family. Across a real strong, rather high fence, I don't know, were maybe sixty or seventy graves, "You want us to go over the fence and mow the…"

"Nah. That's Potter's field. Those gravestones don't even have names."

"Well, who were those people?"

"Who cares? They died in jail, died paupers, died without family. Don't mow there, just let the weeds grow." No names. Why show up if you don't have a name?

One time I was having a chaplain's retreat, a preaching workshop or something for chaplains, at Fort Belvoir, in Virginia. Oh, they treated me real nice. I ate in the, what do you call it, officers' mess or something like that, where the officers ate. The soldiers waiting on us wore that kind of sad green fatigue-type clothing, but there where every soldier had a name tag, there was nothing. That little thing had been ripped off. The fellow waiting on me was very nice and all, and I said, "I see you don't have on your name tag. What's your name?" He didn't answer me. So I said to the officer beside me, "Why doesn't he answer? What's his name?"

The officer said, "He doesn't have one."

"What do you mean? Give me a break here. What's his name?"

"He has no name."

"He *has* a name." No, no, no, no. I said, "Who are these people waiting on us?"

"Conscientious objectors in the Vietnam War. Conscientious objectors, they don't exist; they have no names. Eat your lunch."

I recall some years ago in a church I was visiting on a Sunday afternoon, a van pulled up in the church parking lot, and a bunch of young people got out. They looked like thirteen, fourteen, fifteen, maybe up to eighteen years old. I think there were ten or twelve young people who belonged to that church. They got out with bedrolls. It was the awfullest looking bunch of kids you've ever seen, something like the cats would drag in. They were really in bad shape. I said, "What is this?" They had just returned from a work mission. They named the place where they went. In one week, those young people, along with other young people, had built a little church for a community. They were beat. Aw, they looked terrible.

They were sitting on their bags out there waiting for their parents to come. I said to one of the boys, I said, "You tired?" And he said, "Whew—am I tired!" Then he said, "This is the best tired I've ever felt."

Now that's what joy is. Do you feel that? "This is the best tired I've ever felt." I hope some day young people in this church get that tired. I hope we all get that tired. The best tired there is, is called in your Bible, joy.

I recall being in a church to preach on a Sunday evening, and still in the pew was a bulletin from Sunday morning. I noticed the pastor that morning had preached on the title "Eating Soup with an Axe." I didn't have a clue, and I don't imagine he did or the people who heard that.

Up in our area, when we lived near Knoxville, a church advertised, or at least the minister advertised, the sermon on a given Sunday: "What's Under the Bed Sheet?" There was a huge crowd. You couldn't see for the people: they were in the aisles, they used chairs, they were standing at the back. People came. At the appointed time in the service when the minister was to stand and preach, two of the men of the church rolled out a chalkboard with a sheet in front. The sheet was lifted, and there was an outline of his sermon. A lot of disappointed, deceived people. Have to be careful with these attention getters.

Pastor of our home church, years ago, advertised on a given Sunday he was going to preach "The Member of this Church I Would Most Like to See in Hell." Boy, did we have a crowd! People who'd never been came. It was fantastic. A bunch of us kids, boys from the Sunday school class, were sitting back there, all anxious to see who it was. Finally, when he called the name—he actually called the name—it was our Sunday school teacher. And we said, "Yeah." No, no, we didn't really. Then he went on to say that the reason he had chosen her to be the one he would most like to see in hell was because she was such a quality saint that, within two weeks, hell would be converted. And it made a nice sermon, but people, you know, still were expecting something else.

I told you about that minister when I was preaching in that church in Louisville. He said, "Now you go on down by the choir, and I'll join you up there." I thought he was going to have a prayer at the back. He disappeared. Later in the service, things were going along, and I was wondering where he was, when the window opened. He crawled in through the window. He came up, sat up there through the whole service, and acted like a fairly decent human being. I asked him later, I said, "What'd you do that for?"

He said, "Well, everybody just sits out there so bored. I thought I'd give them a little something extra."

Now there was a church in my hometown that insisted the members show that they were different. The women could not wear any cosmetics; could not wear any kind of jewelry, earrings or necklaces; could not cut their hair; could not wear short-sleeved dresses; could not in any way show that they were like other people. There was a family of several girls that were about my grade in school, and I remember what a painful thing it was for them to come to school looking sort of like their own grandmothers—long dresses, long-sleeved blouses, hot as everything, tied up to here, and no makeup, no cutting of the hair.

There was one that broke away from the group. I remember the year she did it. She went into the girls' restroom—I wasn't in there, of course—but what she apparently did was to roll up the waistband of her skirt so it was the same length as everybody else's. She undid the blouse, opened the collar of the blouse, rolled up the sleeves, put on some eye shadow and some lipstick, and she pulled that long hair up on her head and parked it behind her right ear. And she came out of there looking like everybody else. That afternoon, when the bell rang to go home, she went in there and came out looking like she was expected to look in her church and in her home.

When Nettie and I were in Ireland, we noticed behind the farmers' homes and cottages, little yards fenced in, and there'd be a donkey back there in the backyard, like some people would have a dog. You'd say to the people in the cottage, "Well, you're still using a donkey to work the peat fields?"

"Oh, no, no, we have a motorized plow now to work the field."

"Well, we saw you still have the donkey."

"Oh, yeah, the donkey pulled our plow and cut our peat, for six years. We don't need the donkey now, but we're not going to run the donkey off or sell it. That donkey's a part of the family. Our children would kill us if we did something to that donkey."

"You mean you just keep it back there, and feed it, and take care of it, and have the veterinarian..."

"Yeah, yeah."

"Well, doesn't that cost?"

"Yeah, yeah, yeah. What's the alternative? We love this donkey."

Sometimes beyond the practical, to the level of love, the rules change so much that you would risk even a great deal to take care of the animal.

Once when we were in Oklahoma, they announced a tornado was coming. We stood out in the front yard and watched the tornado, and the weatherman was right—it was coming. We watched it move, and we thought it would change directions. Then we saw that it was not going to change directions, it was going to get our house. So we said we needed to get in the car and drive west of town quickly. We cranked up the car and started out the driveway. "Oh, no! Where's Gretchen?" Gretchen was this little old sausage dog; she was old. She wouldn't bring anything on the market. Here comes a tornado, and we take time to go back in and get Gretchen. Now we're reaching the level of stupidity.

The shepherd had a little enclosure out in the desert. He brings the sheep in, but there are wolves and there are cougars. The shepherd lies down across the gate thinking, *Anything that gets to the sheep will have to come by me.* Now we're approaching something hard. What's the name for this? The name for it is love.

I'll never forget, I've mentioned it to some of you once before, in that service in North Carolina, a big rally of Christian people, we had a preacher there who served as pastor to a church of several thousand— remarkable voice, remarkable sense of humor and stories, and grasp of scripture. He had an immense audience and was at the peak of his performance as a public speaker. This little woman came up to the platform afterward and said, "We're going to have to pray for the speaker."

"Well, of course we'll pray for the speaker, but what do you have in mind?"

She said, "He has real problems."

How did she know that in a motel room fifteen miles away he had brought the other woman. How did she know, this little old woman? I think I know how she knew. She knew the shepherd, and she could tell a stranger.

Nettie and I got acquainted in Chautauqua, New York, with a minister who had no arms. He was born with nothing from here. No arms. He was telling us one day there at Chautauqua the experience of learning to put on his own clothes without any arms. He said his mother always dressed him, and he'd gotten to be a pretty big boy. She fed him, she dressed him, she fed him, she dressed him. One day she put his clothes in the middle of the floor and said, "Dress yourself."

He said, "I can't dress myself, I don't have..."

She said, "You'll have to dress yourself," and she left the room.

He said, "I kicked, I screamed, I kicked, I screamed, I yelled, 'You don't love me anymore!' Finally, I realized that, if I were to get any clothes on, I'd have to get my clothes on." After hours of struggle, he got some clothes on. He said, "It was not until later that I knew my mother was in the next room crying."

I don't know if God distances God's self from us, but I know sometimes we feel some distance.

There are places everybody just ought to go. Like to Washington. You know, we took our grandkids this past summer to Washington, and it was a remarkable time. I told them to study and get ready. When we got there, I said, "Well, what did you read?" None of them had read anything. I said, "Well, then, do you know anything?" Oh, yeah, yeah. See, they got it off the Internet. Whatever happened to reading? Whatever happened to good books? Well, at any rate…They were ready, and we had a "cool" trip. There were a lot of things we saw that the grandkids would say, "Cool; hey, this is cool; this is really cool." I got a little tired of "cool." But it was cool.

But there were some places that were not "cool." They were quiet— Ford's Theatre and the box where Lincoln was shot, and the house across the street where he died; Kennedy's grave; the changing of the guard at Arlington Cemetery. Those were quiet places. The Vietnam Wall was a quiet place, as were the Korean Memorial, the Nurses' Memorial, the Lincoln Monument. Oh, that remarkable place. On one wall beside him is the Gettysburg Address, and on the other his second inaugural address. You ought to read it every year. Absolutely remarkable. It was a good trip. There are some things you just have to do at the places where it happened.

I recall when I was a youngster and had, for a long period of time, malaria. I turned yellow and sweaty, took quinine, and was quarantined. Nobody could come in the house, and I couldn't go outside. All the other kids and my brothers and my sisters were out playing, and I was confined to the house and feeling miserable. On one occasion I suppose I was whining a little much, and my father came into the room, and he told me two things.

The first thing was, there is no way to modulate the human voice to make a whine acceptable. The second thing he said to me was, even if you spend the rest of your life in a wheelchair or in bed, it can be a full and good life. What was he talking about? How is that possible? It is possible because you become the temple of God in which God lives and gives abundant life and joy to you and to me.

If I have more than my usual otherworldly glow, I need to explain. This past week I went to see *Star Wars, Episode 1, The Phantom Menace*. We went with our grandsons, daughter, and son-in-law from Oklahoma. I was determined to take them to see this, even though when I arrived, they said, "We've seen this, but you have to see it lots of times."

I said, "Okay." I didn't want to be totally ignorant, so I inquired around before going, to find something about it, and I had the name Luke Skywalker. That's about all I had. We went to this crowded theater, mostly people in their thirties, I would guess. The thing started, and in just a few minutes there was loud applause. I mean, we had just gotten there. I asked the boys what the applause was for, and they said, "Those two are Jedi."

I said, "Well, of course." As it went on, it became increasingly clear that I didn't know anything about it, so I asked my ten-year-old grandson next to me, "When is Luke Skywalker going to come in?"

He said, "He hasn't been born yet."

I said, "Well, I had that name, Luke Skywalker, and he was a good guy."

He said, "Well, episodes 4, 5, and 6 came out, and now we're going to have 1, 2, and 3."

I said, "That's why everybody in here knows so much."

He said, "Yeah. Everybody knows that. We have them at home if you want to look at them."

I said, "Well, thanks, um, I don't think so." Later, I said, "That's rather strange, having episode 1 after you've had 4, 5, and 6."

And he said, "Uh, Gramps, this is a prequel. A prequel. It's before the others."

I said, "All right."

But when he said that, I was immediately at home, because that's the way the Bible is. You know the end before the beginning. The resurrection shines back through every story, including the birth story. The light of the resurrection is on the manger. You know the end before the beginning. I said, "Hey, I'm into this." And I thought, *I know the sequel.*

There are churches everywhere, grand cathedrals that take your breath away; beautiful brick and stone and wood buildings; cinder block buildings; and simple, inexpensive, grass huts, igloos, and brush arbors. Everywhere in the world you go, somebody is reading the Bible and worshiping God and learning about Jesus. That's the sequel. Now, what's the prequel? Our text is the prequel. This is the prequel. In other words, this is the way it started. The risen Christ, on an unnamed mountain, an uncharted mountain in the north of Israel in Galilee, met with the eleven.

When we lived in Oklahoma, our neighbor up the street, still a young man, was killed in a crash. While the crepe was still on the door, here came a red-hot evangelist from some church and rang our doorbell. I went to the door. He said, "Do you know what happened to him up the street?"

I said, "Yes, and it's very sad. We're all torn up about it."

"Well, what about *your* soul?"

Throughout my ministry, I've had the occasion to go to camp and conference in the summer with young people, junior high and senior high age. We'd meet on Sunday evening with them and go through all of that together—fun and laugh and have a good time. There was a session where somebody asked me, one of the kids, "Um, I don't know, I don't know how to ask this, but, uh, did Jesus ever say anything about sex? And if he did, what'd he say?" She wants to know what Jesus said. "Well, I've been told by a lot of people that I should make my life what God would have it to be. How can I know what that is? How can I know?"

She said, "A friend of mine in my class at school committed suicide, and her minister said it was the unpardonable sin. What do you think? Did Jesus say anything about suicide?" Do you know, she's fourteen years old, and asking me what Jesus said about suicide?

"They" are wrong, they are flat wrong to think that all young people want is entertainment. What did Jesus say? This kind of floozied-up fifteen-year-old, trying to impress me as twenty-two, hung around after everybody, and she said, "Will I go to hell for not wanting to go to heaven?"

"Well, um, why? Why are you asking me that?"

She said, "Well, my mother is always yelling. I'll leave the house to go to my friend's here and go to my friend's there, and she's always saying, 'Now if you do so-and-so, and so-and-so, and so-and-so, you're not going to go to heaven.' And I just, well, don't want to go to heaven."

I said, "Why?"

And she said, "Well, it sounds kind of boring. I mean, what do you do?" Fifteen years old, dressed like twenty-two, and asking me about heaven.

I was going through Etowah, Tennessee, at two o'clock in the morning. The sign said "City Limit, 30 Miles an Hour," so I came down to thirty. It was two o'clock in the morning, and I know about those constables sitting around wanting something to do. I was under thirty. Here he comes and pulls me over. I said, "Officer, I was not going thirty miles an hour."

He said, "I know, but do you see that other little sign down there? 'School Zone, 15 miles an hour.'"

I said, "Officer, it's two o'clock in the morning."

He said, "Does it say, except for two o'clock in the morning?"

Well, no.

I had a debate in the state of Missouri some years ago about a passage of scripture: Whoever believes and is baptized shall be saved. This preacher, redheaded, red beard, and ferocious, said to me, "Do you believe in the Bible?"

"Yeah."

"What does it say? Read it." I read it to the people gathered. He said, "Do you believe that?"

I said, "Well, of course, I believe that. But if you have a case of a child who dies on the seventh day of its life, or the ninth day of its life, it had no chance to believe or be baptized."

"Does it say 'except'?"

I said, "But what about people that don't have all their mental faculties?"

"Does it say 'except'?"

And we went at it, back and forth. I wound up as the bleeding heart liberal who didn't believe the Bible, and he came off looking like the stone statue of truth, holding up the word of Christ.

I remember the first time I went to a minister to talk about something personal; it was tough as toenails. It was hard to go and talk to a minister. I had been baptized about two years. Some fellows that I worked with in a box factory went uptown to get a hot dog or a hamburger for lunch. We had an hour for lunch. I still had on my nail apron, and they had on their nail aprons; we drove nails to make these boxes. We passed a blind man on the sidewalk with his guitar, a sign that said "I'm blind. Please help me," and a tin cup taped to the neck of his guitar. It suddenly occurred to the three of us to play a trick. Each of us took some nails from our nail aprons and dropped them in his tin cup, noisily, and he said, "Thank you, thank you very much. May God bless you. Thank you very much."

That began to eat at me; of all of the ugly, terrible things to do. Well, I couldn't get rid of it, so finally I did what some people do only in desperation; I talked to the minister. I went to the minister and told him what I had done, and he sat up at his desk and said, "Are you aware that this country is in the biggest war of our history?" It was World War II, the last year of it. "People are dying by the hundreds every day; soldiers have been away from their families for years. We don't know how this whole thing is going, people dying, starving. And you are worried about nails in a blind man's cup?" He let me go.

My little problem was swallowed up in the problems of the world, but it wouldn't go. Finally, I went to the youth minister, Mignonne. We didn't pay her, but she was a minister. I told her what I had done, and she told me that was a terrible, terrible thing to do. She felt bad, like I felt bad, and she said, "God forgives you for that, but why don't you next week when you have your lunch hour, why don't you go to that same blind man and tell him what you did and ask him to forgive you, and then if you have a nickel or a dime or a quarter, give it to him." I did, and that poor man forgave me, and he smiled and said, "I know how it is. Lot of boys are full of mischief, aren't they?" He forgave me. I had been baptized already, and I was carrying that around.

Now that may not seem big to you, but think about what you're carrying around right now. Would you like to get rid of it?

Some years ago, I was invited to preach at the Riverside Church, New York City. I was in tall cotton. Dr. William Sloane Coffin was the preacher. He had to go somewhere and said, "Fred, come and preach for me." I took a plane from Atlanta. I was in New York City. He said, "You can stay in my apartment—I'm not there." I found the way, found a superintendent at the apartment house, he gave me the key, and I went up to the rather modest apartment where he lived.

But just down the street was this enormous church, one of the most influential, powerful churches in the United States. Harry Emerson Fosdick preached there for years, the great preacher, at Riverside Church. There was nothing in the refrigerator, the next day was Sunday morning, and I needed a little nourishment, you know, this was big. There was a note on the refrigerator door, "If you usually eat breakfast, you can go to the church, we have a breakfast for the homeless people." Well, I walked down the street, this was in a dangerous part of New York, but it was already daylight. It was early, and I walked down there and stood in this line of maybe two hundred people with the metal trays being served in the basement of that church. I talked to the people in front of me, and behind me, and to the people across from me. "Well, what's put you in this situation?"

"Well," he said, "it's alcohol. Might as well be honest with you, it's alcohol. But I'm dry now, I'm dry now."

"What put you...?"

"It was a woman. She took it all."

"Really?"

"Yeah."

"What put you here?" one of them asked me.

"I was invited," I said. I didn't know how to answer them. I didn't want to create any distance, so I just ate what they ate, talked with them, then went back to the room.

Church time, so I went up there and put on my robe with all my stripes on it and stuff. I stood up in that beautiful pulpit, with hundreds and hundreds of people out there worshiping, the enormous choir, the organ filled the front of the church—it just gave goose bumps on goose bumps. I was in the pulpit of Riverside Church, New York City. And I said to myself, *Who am I?* I'm a guest, a guest of God, a guest of Christ, a guest of the church.

-→═◦✛◦═←-

In the parking lot of the grocery store the other day, I watched a small drama unfold. It involved as principal characters two fellows I would regard as brothers. One seemed to be maybe nineteen, the other I would guess to be twelve years old. I say they were brothers—they looked alike, talked alike, and the way they talked to each other, they had to be brothers. The younger one was over at the front of the store, trying to get a drink out of the pop machine. He yelled over to his older brother in the parking lot, saying, "I put my money in and didn't get anything."

The older brother said, "Go inside and tell the lady. She'll give you your money."

He said, "I think I can get it out," and he started beating and banging on the machine. Finally, he grew quiet, and the older brother out in the parking lot said, "Now what have you done?"

He said, "I put in another dollar."

"Well, why did you do that?"

"Well, I thought it would push it out."

"You put in another dollar?"

"Yeah."

"Well, go tell the lady, but she's only going to give you one dollar."

"Why? I put in two."

"Well, she won't believe anybody's that stupid, and she won't give you but one." He went inside, and pretty soon he came out with a pop.

"She wouldn't give me any money, but she gave me a pop."

The older brother had troubles of his own. He was out in the parking lot walking around a small, I would say '94, '95 Ford Escort, blue, with a temporary sticker in the back window, North Carolina. He was kicking the tires and banging on the trunk of it and making all kinds of useless commotion. I got out of my vehicle and I said, "Can I help you?"

He said, "I've locked my keys in there. Just bought this today over in Murphy."

I said, "Well, I don't even have a coat hanger to help you. Sometimes you can get a coat hanger down there."

He said, "No, I have a coat hanger. I tried that, but I've already called my buddy. He's coming, and we'll get it open," and he kicked the tires, and he walked around and beat on it.

I said, "Well, if I had one of those Slim Jims, but I don't have anything. A few years ago, I locked mine in there, and it cost me thirty dollars, but at least I got them out. I'd be glad to call…"

"Nah, I don't want to spend any money on it. My buddy's coming."

So I got back in the vehicle and watched and observed and listened as people came by to give him advice. The first car that pulled up was a truck. "You need to get yourself an extra set of keys."

He said, "Well, I plan to, but I just bought this today. I haven't had time."

Next car came by. "What's the matter?"

"Locked my keys in there."

"You need to have one of those things you can push down by the window, and then you can get…"

"Well, I don't have one. If I did, I would already have it open," and it went on.

Someone else stopped by and said, "If that were a Toyota, I could show you how to get it open."

He said, "It's a Ford," and they went on.

And then someone came by, just before I left, and said, "Is that your car?"

He said, "You think I'm trying to break in a car? Sure it's my car," and they went on by.

What happened to the day? Here's a young man, late teens. Bought himself a car. Picked up his younger brother. Went to Blue Ridge. Pulled into the shopping center and was grounded. He didn't plan it that way. What happened? Life happened.

I had a friend when we were in Columbia, Tennessee, who was the pastor of the largest church in town, and in many ways he was a very successful minister, except his church was full of problems. Whatever you said or did, is the way he reported it to me, there was a big problem. He got so sick and tired of it. I saw him downtown one day and I said, "How's it going?"

He said, "Terrible. I'm thinking of quitting."

"Aw, you're not going to…"

"Why not?"

"Oh, you don't want to quit."

He said, "You know what I'm going to do? I'm going to buy a little piece of land over in Arkansas in a rice field, and I'm going to build my own church. It's going to be a study where I can do my work, and it'll have a beautiful tall spire, and that'll be it. No sanctuary. No Sunday school rooms. No fellowship hall. No members. Just me and God."

Clean up the rolls. It's a natural inclination, but the difficult part, the difficult part of this story is that the boss said, "Leave the weeds alone."

Some of you remember Paul Culpepper. He was a preacher in these parts for seventy years. A wonderful man, full of stories about his ministry that went back, you know, forever. He was telling one day about his holding a revival meeting across the line in Tennessee in Polk County. The minister came to him before the meeting started that Sunday night, and he said, "Now, we're going to have to do something at the beginning."

"Well, what's that?"

"We're going to have to call for the fellowship and peace of the church."

"Why?"

"Well, I'm the one that's done wrong. You know, I'm a married man, got a good family and all, but I asked a certain widow in this town for a date. I shouldn't have done it. She turned me down, but then she went and told everybody. Now, that's all over the church and that's all over town. So, you have to call for the fellowship and peace of the church."

And Paul said, "I did. At the close of the service…"

Do you know what calling for the peace and fellowship is? Well, I have to explain everything here. Everybody sits down, and then the minister says, "All who are in true fellowship and peace with God and each other, please stand." Well, just about everybody stood, except the pastor of the church. They all sat down, and then he stood. "Everybody knows what I did. It was wrong, and I regret it. I've been wringing my heart out in sorrow and regret, but I want you to forgive me. I don't have to tell you what it was; you know what it was."

Well, the presider said, "Is there a motion that we forgive the brother?"

And one man stood up and said, "I move we forgive him. I've done the same thing a dozen times!" His wife looked at him, and everybody looked around at him. Well, they forgave the preacher, but then they had to have another meeting to forgive the one who said, "But I didn't mean it that way, I didn't mean it literally."

But that triggered something else. Paul Culpepper said, "We had two weeks not of revival, but of weed-pulling."

Did you read about it? I don't know if I read it or heard it. A young minister in Virginia was telling me about a church down the street from him that weeded its membership. There was a girl, a pretty girl, a member of that church according to his telling, a teenager, wild as a March hare. She did it all, and she was only about fifteen or sixteen, and she had been there and back a lot of times. Well, it was an embarrassment to the church and all, and so they met, and they weeded her over it. They said she was not to come in to the church building, sing, listen, pray, give offering, or take communion for twelve months. It tore the church up. It tore up two or three families. It tore up the town. "Leave the weeds alone!"

You can't teach an old dog new tricks. Wrong. If you believe in God, you can teach an old dog new tricks. I've never been to the greyhound races, but I've seen them on TV. They have these beautiful, big old dogs—I say beautiful, they're really ugly—big old dogs, and they run that mechanical rabbit around the ring, and these dogs just run, exhausting themselves chasing it. When those dogs get to where they can't race, the owners put a little ad in the paper, and if anybody wants one for a pet, they can have it, otherwise they're going to be destroyed. I have a niece in Arizona who can't stand that ad. She goes and gets them. Big old dogs in the house; she loves them.

I was in a home not long ago where they'd adopted a dog that had been a racer. It was a big old greyhound, spotted hound, lying there in the den. One of the kids in the family, just a toddler, was pulling on its tail, and a little older kid had his head over on that old dog's stomach, used it for a pillow. That dog just seemed so happy, and I said to the dog, "Uh, are you still racing any?"

"No, no, no, I don't race anymore."

I said, "Do you miss the glitter and excitement of the track?"

He said, "No, no."

I said, "Well, what's the matter? You got too old?"

"No, no, I still had some race in me."

"Well, did you not win?"

He said, "I won over a million dollars for my owner."

"Then what was it, bad treatment?"

"Oh, no, they treated us royally when we were racing."

I said, "Then what? Did you get crippled?"

He said, "No, no, no."

I said, "Then what?"

And he said, "I quit."

"You quit?"

Yeah, that's what he said. "I quit."

I said, "Why did you quit?"

And he said, "I discovered that what I was chasing was not really a rabbit. And I quit." He looked at me and said, "All that running, running, running, running, and what I was chasing, not even real."

When I read that story in which the woman hid the yeast in the dough, I think of the little church in Jeff, Illinois. You don't know about Jeff, Illinois. It's just practically no community at all, no village at all, and one little church, the Jeff Christian Church. They didn't have enough members to get a good minister. The ministers would come who were just starting out, and sometimes they would get an old minister who should've retired a long time ago, but that was sort of it. Usually they had Sunday school, had the Lord's supper, sang a hymn, and left. Sometimes had a sermon. Little church. The coal stove hardly heated the little building out there in the corn field. It didn't amount to anything. It's gone now, couldn't make it. But out of the church in Jeff, Illinois, came young people as missionaries, missionary doctors, ministers, and professors in Christian universities. The total service to Jesus Christ by young people going out of Jeff Church is over 225 years. And you drive by there, and you say, "I wonder if they're having service? I don't see anyone." Hidden.

I'm a little nervous about talking to you from this text, because a former student of mine preached on this text and was fired the next week. It wasn't the sermon, I'm told. His good friend related it to me, but it was what happened after the sermon. I'm sure it was a good sermon. He was a bright student, full of promise, and had a good reputation as a preacher. He had gone to his first church, somewhere in Florida. He preached on this text, and following the sermon and benediction, his wife stood up and said, "I know it comes as a surprise, but I would like for all the congregation to come over to the parsonage for lunch." The parsonage was next door. Well, quite a few went. Why not? When they got over there, she opened the refrigerator and took out and put on the dining table what was in the refrigerator. It wasn't much—a shriveled pickle, carrot or two, few eggs, slice or two of bacon, quart of milk, some hot dog buns, couple of slices of baloney, what was left of a head of lettuce, half a jar of boysenberry jam, that was about it. She asked her husband, the minister, to have a prayer to multiply the food. He prayed, and then they opened their eyes, and the food was just like it was before. She asked him to pray again, and he prayed again, and the food had not multiplied. During the third prayer, everybody left except the minister and his wife.

The next week the board met and fired him. Why? Why did they fire him? Lack of faith? If lack of faith will get you fired, none of us could hold a job. A failed miracle? Maybe that was it. Well, at least he tried. I don't remember ever trying to do a miracle. Unless everything we do is. At least, at least he believed that the things that used to happen can still happen. Things that are recorded in the Bible are not just yesterday; surely God is still able to provide and to do what God did. Was it because the church was embarrassed in the community, that word spread?

By Monday morning the word was out, over the cups of coffee, "Did you hear what happened down at such-and-such church?" And the church, I'm sure, was embarrassed. That might've been it. I don't know. It might have been the audacity to try and duplicate what Jesus did when it was not even to a hungry mob in a desert. They were folk who were going to the restaurants anyway, have a nice meal, watch the ball game. It's kind of nerve-wracking, really. I don't get that close to miracles myself.

I remember as a youngster in the church, the first time a missionary came from the Congo in Africa, it was an agricultural missionary. We'd had evangelists and teachers and, for the first time, we started sending agricultural missionaries. What did they do? They taught the people to feed themselves. This couple, this bright, fun couple, explained to our congregation that when they went to that village where they were, the scrawny little chickens that picked in the street laid about an egg and a half in a year. Not fit to eat, just little sinewy things. So they brought in a new way to raise chickens and a new strain of chickens. In a few years they had big, plump chickens for the table, and they had dozens and dozens of eggs. They could sell eggs, and they could sell chickens, and they were just doing great.

And when the talk was over, somebody in our church said, "I'm not sending any money to missions anymore—over there raising chickens. We gave our money for them to go over there and save souls! Raising chickens. I'm not giving another dime to that." Anybody have a clue about the way some people think?

I lived near a railroad track as a boy, and I remember a number of mornings getting awake, getting up, going into the kitchen to get some breakfast, and there'd be a strange, ugly looking, poorly dressed man at the table eating—just eating away, eating away. I was scared of him. And when he left, I would say, "Mom, who was that?"

She'd say, "Well, his name was Henry, and he said he was hungry."

"Well, where'd he come from?"

"He came down the railroad tracks."

People called them hobos. They walked the tracks begging, maybe stealing, getting what they could to stay alive. They'd stop by our house, and there, sitting in the kitchen eating what we had to eat, just eating it like they'd never have another meal. And I'd say, "Mama, weren't you scared?"

She said, "He's hungry."

"Well, I was scared of him!"

"Well, he was hungry."

Those women from Central Avenue Christian Church that came to our house and brought a pair of Buster Brown shoes that fit me, and enabled me to start Sunday school—those women didn't just bring me a pair of shoes. You know what else they brought? They brought me a picture book of stories about Jesus.

I needed those shoes. I really needed those stories.

I've met a desperate person since we've moved to the mountain. It is a woman. I had gone to the hospital in Fannin County to visit someone else. I didn't know her, didn't know I would encounter her, but when I went down the corridor, I saw her. Her head was against the door, and both fists were up beside her face, and she was banging on the door: "Let me in, let me in, let me in!" I couldn't imagine someone locking her out of the room. I got there, and it was the chapel door.

I said, "Let me help you." I tried to open the door, but the knob wouldn't turn. It was locked. I stopped a worker, and I said, "The chapel is locked."

She said, "We have to keep it locked. There were some kids in here some time ago, and they trashed the chapel. We had to get all new furniture and paint the room. We can't afford to keep doing that, so we keep it locked."

"Well, find someone with a key."

She came back a little bit later with another woman, who opened the door for us, and this woman and I went in. I would say she was about forty. She had the look of desperation. I could tell that she hadn't come to the hospital with any planning; she came urgently, she came running. The dress she had on was not typical public wear. She had no shoes, just scuffs. Her hair had not been combed, no makeup. She had the look of desperation. She had the voice of desperation. I can't tell you if she was screaming or crying or moaning or what it was, but it was desperation. Strange sound. I heard some of her words. "I know he's going to die, I know he's going to die, I know he's going to die."

"Who?"

"My husband."

"What's the matter?"

"He's had a heart attack."

I said, "Can I get you some water?"

She said, "No."

I told her who I was, and I said, "Can I pray with you?"

And she said, "Please."

I started to pray for her and for her husband, and she interrupted me. She didn't just interrupt me; she took over. She started praying herself and stopped my prayer. I think maybe I was too quiet or too slow or saying the wrong thing or something. Anyway, my prayer wasn't getting there, and she knew it. So she said, "Lord, this is not the time to take my husband. You know that better than I do, he's not ready. Never prays, never goes to church or anything. He's not ready, not a good time to take him. Don't take him now. And what about me? If I have to raise these kids, what am I going to do? I don't have any skills, can't find any work. I quit school to marry him. If I'd have known you were going to take him, I'd have stayed in school." She was really talking to God. "And what about the kids? They don't mind me now with him around. If he's gone, they'll be wild as bucks. What about the kids? This is not the time to take my husband." Whew.

I stayed as long as I felt useful. I went back the next morning, and she had on a nice dress; she had on shoes; she had combed her hair. She looked fine. She was in the hallway outside intensive care. Before I could ask, she said, "He's better." She smiled and said, "I'm sorry about that crazy woman yesterday."

I said, "Well, you weren't crazy."

She said, "I guess the Lord heard one of us."

I said, "He heard you."

She was desperate. She had God by the lapels, both hands, and was screaming in God's face: "I don't think you're listening!" That's desperation.

I recall how difficult it was for me. After all these years, it's still very vivid. We went five miles in the country into town to school. My brother and I rode Bess, our family mare, to school. We were sort of laughed at, riding a horse to school. I was poorly clothed, with chronic malaria, not very well, not very strong, undersized. That was before I achieved the stature that you are admiring before you now. And I was very noncompetitive. I did not compete with any of the others for the teacher's attention—I didn't understand why they wanted it. The pencil sharpener was up by her desk, and some children, "Can I sharpen my pencil please? May I come up and..." Some of them chewed up their pencils just to go up and be close to the teacher. "May I go to the restroom?" and they'd go out right beside the teacher. I never sharpened my pencil; I never went to the restroom. I sat in the back, easily hidden. And I counted it a very successful day when I was not called on, I was not noticed, nobody knew I was there. I thought that was a perfect day. I had a lot of those perfect days, because back when I was in school, teachers had a tendency, if a child didn't make a lot of noise or cause any trouble, if a child was quiet, the teacher wrote down, "Good child." They didn't know that I was plotting revolution back there. We have finally learned that the quiet child may be near explosion. But because I was quiet, very seldom was I called on; very seldom did I hear my name, and I celebrated that.

But in the third grade, there was a torture instrument that would enter my life called the "recitation bench." Now, this is ancient history, just stay with me. The recitation bench was a bench in the front of the classroom, and we were brought to the recitation bench about six or eight at a time, to recite. The teacher would call your name, and you'd stand up. The whole class is in there—the teacher and the others. She would give you a question. You'd stand. "What's seven times seven?" "What's the capital of Idaho?" I don't know why she asked that. She'd been to college, or she could look it up. But she kept asking, "What's the capital of Idaho?" I dreaded it when she called my name; I was called by my middle name in those days, Brenning. "Brenning!" I would stand, and she would ask me some question. We recited poetry also; we memorized poetry. "Fourteen Hundred Ninety Two, Columbus sailed the ocean blue." You remember the poetry you recited? "Listen, my children, and you shall hear of the midnight ride of Paul Revere; Seventeen Hundred and Seventy Five, there's hardly a man now alive who remembers that famous day and year." You remember that? "Whenever the moon and stars are set, whenever the wind is high; all night long through the dark and wet, a man goes riding by." I never had trouble, really, with the numbers. I never had trouble with the capital of Idaho. I never had trouble with the poems. What I had trouble with was having to stand up in front of everybody and say it out loud. It was painful.

But for all the pain of the recitation bench, there was nothing so painful as church. You see, on the recitation bench, you got to just report on other people. Abraham Lincoln, Meriwether Lewis, Charles Lindbergh. No sweat, really. I just hated to have to get up there, but I knew all those reports. But in church…

That's the thing about church. You can't just report on what everybody else is saying; you've got to say something yourself. It's really hard. I remember the Sunday I believed what the preacher said. I'd gotten to where I was listening. I quit passing notes and popping bubble gum, and I quit talking and fumbling and fidgeting. I started listening. I was fourteen, and I listened. I was concerned about the things in the Bible, and I wanted to know, and I wanted to be a part of it. I wanted to be baptized.

But the preacher said, "You'll have to say something in front of the people." What's the report? Oh, it's not recitation bench, this is confession of faith. The Sunday I had chosen to go, there were a bunch of my friends, twelve, thirteen, or fourteen went down, and seven or eight went to the front, and there I was locked in my pew. I looked at the aisle, and it had suddenly become two miles long. "I'll never get down there." I didn't go.

My mother said, "I thought you…"

"Well, I was. Can I just go to the minister's study on Tuesday and tell him?"

"No, no, no."

"'If you confess me before others, I will confess you before my father,' that's what Jesus said."

"Well, I like silence."

Then I shifted into the old silence gear. "You know, silence is golden. Why aren't you saying anything? Well, I, I believe I learn more just listening. I don't learn much when I'm talking." Oh, don't give me that stuff. You know it's not true. "Well, we have one mouth, but we have two ears, supposed to listen twice as much as we speak, and so…" Oh, be quiet. That is not true. You don't even know what you believe until you hear yourself say it.

Charles and Emily were having a dinner party in their home. There were, I think, besides Charles and Emily, maybe eight people, all adults except for their boy, seven-year-old Robbie. We got ready to gather around the table, in fact, had gathered around the table, and Charles said to Emily, "Where's Robbie?"

She said, "I think he's outside." She went to the back door and called him, and then she went into the backyard, then came running back, and said, "Charles, do something! He has a snake!"

Charles said, "You shouldn't interfere with a boy growing up."

She said, "But it's a snake."

He said, "Emily, our guests are ready for the meal. Let's be seated."

We were seated. He had the blessing: "Bless this food to our bodies, use us to thy service. Amen," and we started eating. I wanted him to call on me for the blessing, because I was going to include a little prayer for Robbie.

Robbie came in after a little bit, and his dad said, "Go wash up, Robbie. Always wash your hands after you've been handling snakes." Charles was right, you know. You shouldn't interfere with a child's growing up, protecting them always from the bruises and the pain and the disappointments and the tears that are going to come. Just let them get up, brush themselves off, and get back up in the saddle, get back on the bicycle. You can't move the wall; don't protect them if they're headed for the wall. They hit the wall, and so they learn. Charles was right.

But Emily was right, because it was a snake! What kind of snake? He didn't know what kind of snake—it was a snake. And she was right, that sometimes the danger is too great, sometimes the price is too high. This is a question, of course, every parent deals with every day. Should I or should I not interfere?

I'll never forget the day Barbara Jenkins walked in the room. It was at a reception of some sort, you know? I don't remember the occasion. There was a punch bowl, and a bowl of salted peanuts, little mints, some of those little triangle sandwiches, you know? There was pimento cheese, tuna fish, ham—really nice, but you had to eat a lot to make anything out of it. Standing around, having a lot of conversation, but not really important. "Could use some more rain."

"Yeah, need some more rain. It's been pretty hot too, cooling off, getting close to fall now."

"You watch the game?"

And then Barbara Jenkins came in. There was something about the room that changed when she came in. "Who is Barbara Jenkins?"

"That's Barbara?"

"Yeah, that's Barbara Jenkins."

Barbara Jenkins spends her time writing letters, making calls, going and seeing folk to make a difference in the way the law treats juvenile offenders. Night and day, seven days a week she worries the authorities to death. "You enjoy doing that?"

"Well, not really."

"You get paid? Are you on salary?"

"No, no, no."

"You have children in trouble with the law and you want…"

"No, no, no."

"Then why in the world? It's no fun; you're not making any money; none of your friends are doing it."

And she says, "I have to."

Got back last night, still a little tired, from two days with the Christian Churches of South Carolina at their regional assembly at Antioch Christian Church in Varnville, way down there in the low country of South Carolina. I had a wonderful time. It was the hundred and twenty-first assembly of the Christian Churches of South Carolina. It was the first time they met in a black church. For years after the Civil War, they had two assemblies, one for whites, one for blacks. And finally they got the gumption to say, "We should all just be in one assembly. We're all brothers and sisters in Christ." So they did, but they always held it, for 100 years, in white churches. This was the first year, the hundred and twenty-first year, they had it in a black church. It was the largest attendance anybody there could remember, great food, great fellowship, good program, good spirit, everybody hugging and kissing and saying, "Why did it take us a hundred and twenty-one years to do this? What's the matter with us anyway?" They asked me to work while I was there. They said, "We want you to preach in a worship service, we want you to give a Bible study of about an hour, and we want you to speak at our fellowship meal." I didn't have a whole lot of time.

In order to clear my head and regroup, I would go outside, and once I even got in the car and drove around to get my gears shifted for the next occasion. As I was driving around—this is a rural church, about six miles out from the little town there—I saw an old cemetery, and I like cemeteries. Everybody should spend a little time with their own generation. So I went to the cemetery. I wanted to see how old some of the graves were. I like to look and see if a lot of the deaths occurred in the same year and wonder if it was an epidemic or if there was a tragedy, a natural disaster or something like that. I was reading markers, and there was this plot with a huge stone, which was the head of the family, the family name, and then a lot of burial plots on either side, stretching out for some distance. This is the low country with shallow soil, much sand, and so for reasons I didn't inquire, but for reasons known to them, they don't just bury and have dirt over the grave, but they have a concrete slab the full length and size of the grave itself.

I was looking at all these, and in this one large plot within the cemetery, belonging obviously to one family, there was the most unusual thing. All the graves were lined up. There were small graves, children and infants, and there were adult graves, quite a few of them, but there was one grave in which the slab was oblique, crosswise, like we used to say, catty-wampus, slanted —and actually took up three burial plots for this one that was at a strange angle. I was pondering that. What a careless thing to do. Maybe some disaster…What was that? A man was walking around in the cemetery, perhaps for the same reason as I was. I said, "Are you from around here?"

And he said, "Yes. You're looking at that grave, aren't you?"

I said, "Yes."

He said, "I knew that fellow." The grave marker said 1994, and he was in his seventies. It was a man. He said, "We were in the same church; I knew him well, knew him all my life."

I said, "Why this burial at an angle?"

"Well, the family wanted that, and the church agreed."

"But why?"

"'Cause that's the kind of guy he was."

I said, "What do you mean, that's the kind of guy he was?"

He said, "He was cross with everything. We never knew him to be pleased about anything, at home or at church. 'Well, why's she doing that?' 'Well, why did they ask him to do that?' 'Well, he's the wrong one to be doing that.' 'Well, I wonder who decided to do that.' All the time. All the time. And the family decided that they wouldn't try to change him just because he was dead, so they buried him crosswise."

I said, "Well, that's an awful thing to do."

He said, "Well, they wanted it to be a witness."

"Okay…"

"The family said, 'If God wants to straighten him out, God can straighten him out! But he left here just like he lived.'"

I've never seen anything like it.

Nettie and I used to have a neighbor across the street. I don't know why I got sucked into it; she'd do it to me every time. She would read the paper to see what was on at the theater in that little town. She'd say, "I noticed such-and-such a movie is on. Have you seen it?"

Sometimes I'd say, "Yes," and then I'd say, "Have you seen it?"

And she'd say, "No. I don't think Christians should go to the movies."

She sucked me in, you see. Now what I finally caught on to was this: She got more pleasure out of not going to the movie than I did in going to the movie, and then she doubled her pleasure by indicting me for going to the movie.

I was once in some town to preach, and they housed me in the little motel there. I had noticed earlier in the day that there was a coffeepot in the lobby, so after I'd finished the evening service and went back a bit weary, I went into the lobby and said to the woman there, "I'd like to get a cup of coffee and take it to my room."

She said, "There's not any."

I looked over, and there wasn't any. I said, "Oh, it's all gone?"

She said, "I didn't make any."

I said, "Well, I noticed the pot there earlier today, and I thought maybe I could get a cup of coffee."

She said, "When I was a child, my mother used to give us, when we got sick, castor oil, and she would always put it in coffee to get us to take it down. Ever since then I just can't stand the smell of coffee or the taste of coffee, so I didn't make any coffee."

I said, "But you have…"

"Well, the people who used to run this had that there, I don't make…"

"Well, then there's no coffee."

She said, "No coffee here. Maybe some place is open where you can get some coffee."

And I said, "Well, I sure hope it's run by somebody whose mother didn't give castor oil in coffee."

See, I didn't know that until she told me the reason she didn't fix coffee for anybody was her mother. You never know.

I remember when Mrs. Foster—you don't know Mrs. Foster—when her mother was dying of cancer, and Mrs. Foster wanted me to come to the house and have prayer and scripture with her mother, which I did. When I got to the house, she handed me a Lutheran prayer book in German. I said, "I thought your mother was United Methodist?"

She said, "She was. She married my father, who was Methodist, and they were together in the church for over forty years."

I said, "What's this?"

And she said, "My mother came from the old country when she was a teenager. She's from Germany, and it would mean a lot to her if you would read the Lord's Prayer in German."

I read to her the Lord's Prayer in German, and that dying woman mouthed the words and smiled.

I told you, didn't I, about that lady, I thought of her this week. I told this group two years ago. I go to Atlanta (well, really to Oxford, Georgia) and share in a southern folk Advent service every year. We have two services. There's a crowd, and so we have to do it twice.

And this woman came, came late with noisy kids. She distracted everybody, disturbed everybody around. Kind of bothered me a little bit, though I can usually just chop right down the row, but they were really a distraction. At the fellowship time afterward, she came up to me and said, "You don't know me, but I'm the one with the noisy kids."

And I said, "Yeah. I noticed when you came in."

We talked a little bit. Next night she was back, without the kids. At the coffee hour she said, "You remember me from last night?"

And I said, "Yeah, you're the one with the noisy kids."

She said, "I didn't bring them tonight."

I said, "Oh, they're not with you?"

She said, "I take noisy kids and go late when I don't want something to get to me. I came without them."

Did she want to be affected by the gospel? No. Yes. No. And then she said, "You won't believe what a mess I've made of my life." Yes.

I remember years ago taking part in a conference at Clemson University in South Carolina. I lectured there, preached in the morning, lectured in the afternoon, and again in the evening. In the evening before I gave my lecture, they had a young woman give the devotional. I didn't know her, didn't know her name, didn't know who she was. She was a young woman, I would say in her mid-twenties, pale, blond, straight hair, thin, no makeup, soft voice. And she got up to have the devotion, and she had one of those legal-length yellow tablets. I thought, *Well, we're here for the night, you know. Everybody, you know, has one sermon.*

Her voice was low, but I am sure I'm right in saying that she was speaking in another language. And then she spoke in another language. And then she spoke in another language. And then she spoke in another language. I don't know how many; I didn't keep count. But what she was doing was saying one thing in the different languages of the world. When she got to German, I thought I knew what she said; when she got to French, I thought I knew what she said. But I really knew what she said when she got to English.

The last time she said it—and I suppose she'd said it sixty or seventy times, one sentence, one sentence—the last was English. She said, "Mommy, I'm hungry." She sat down.

Thought about it all the way back that night. I drove back to Atlanta; I had to teach the next day. The first billboard that I saw going back down the highway going into the north side of Atlanta, the first billboard that I saw said this: "All You Can Eat $5.99." I don't blame them. All you can eat, $5.99. There it was in my head. "Mommy, I'm hungry."

I remember a century ago, when I was in high school, I was quarterback of our little football team. I'm pausing to let the absurdity of that sink in. It was a small school, and a small town, and a small team. Our heaviest guy was 170 pounds. He was our fullback and had all the speed and grace of a spastic turtle. Our team was not any good. We played the towns around, as you do in small towns; we played them and we had our annual competitions.

The town next to us, twelve miles away, had us down at halftime, twenty-one to nothing. We crawled in at the half, into the dressing room, lying around licking our wounds, wishing the game were over. Coach got up as was his custom at the end of the dressing room there to speak to us. We were ready to be chewed out.

He said, "Fellas, I don't have much to say today. I just want to read this to you." He pulled out of his pocket a yellow sheet of paper, and he started to read, and he choked up. He tried to read it again, and he became very emotional. He handed it to an assistant and left the room. We were as quiet as could be. The assistant said, "What the coach wanted to read to you was this telegram he's received. It simply says, 'Win this one for me,' and it's signed 'Joe.'"

We didn't know who Joe was, but the country was at war, and we pictured him in a foxhole somewhere about to be shot, and he had graduated from there, and he had played there. Surely we could win one for Joe. Every guy on the team grew about six inches, put on fifty pounds. We went out there, and we beat them twenty-eight to twenty-one. The local paper carried a notice, kind of a headline, and we were all proud: "It's not the size of the dog in the fight; it's the size of the fight in the dog." Ah, we felt good.

About three or four weeks later, we found out that the coach made up that telegram. There was no Joe, there was no telegram, and he had been using that trick for years. We were let down, but it worked.

I have a former student, Jim Strain, who writes screenplays. He lives out in California, and after several years of starving to death, he's been able to sell some. He's written some movie screenplays and all that. He was in my class on the parables of Jesus, and he says, "Everything I do reflects that class." He wrote a screenplay for the old TV drama called *M*A*S*H*.

You remember M★A★S★H★, that hospital in Korea and all the characters, doctors, and nurses in that military hospital? There is a chaplain in that M★A★S★H unit who is a priest, a Catholic priest. And Jim wrote, he wrote a play involving the priest. And here was the story.

The priest at some point became very attracted to one of the nurses—he was really attracted to that nurse. He had taken the vows of his priesthood, of poverty, chastity, obedience. He was attracted to that nurse. And Jim said that the whole story is about that struggle, that struggle, and finally he says no to her and reaffirms his yes to God. Jim said to me, "I had an awful time selling that script."

"If you'd just change the ending, make it more realistic."

"What would make it more realistic?"

"He goes for the nurse! He disavows his priesthood! Don't you understand what people want?"

And Jim said, "No."

Don't you understand what people want?

Tom Cousins, the big developer in Atlanta, and a strong churchman, North Presbyterian Church, has in recent years, as some of you know, redeveloped the old East Lake district in southeast Atlanta, around that golf course. He redid the golf course, but the housing around it—a project—is a center of crime and drugs and crime and drugs. He got the permission to bulldoze all that and to build new housing. Now, the whole idea was not let's just rebuild bad housing, but let's change the way people think about life, especially the young people. Because in the old housing project, the only successful person, the only successful person the kids in the project ever saw was the drug dealer who came around in a stretch limo, parking at the corners and making his sales. And did he have the money, did he have the money. All those little kids saying, "Now there is success."

Well, in the new project, there's a family on welfare, and then next door to them there's a family that works—nurse, doctor, school-teacher, policeman, insurance salesman—and then you have another welfare family, another family that works, another welfare family, another family that works, and the children are seeing that there are people who make it in the world who are not dealing drugs, holding up before the young people of that project another image.

✦

When I was in Cincinnati, I met a lot of people I was glad to see, and a few I didn't really care to see again, but there they were. One of them was a fellow in one of the churches in the Midwest; I'll not identify him any further. Grumpy sort. A controlling man—that was the problem I had with him. I gave Bible studies and preached in his church lots of times. He's a layman in the church, and a sort of controller, a very controlling man, one of those people that act like they're in the background—"Well, I don't know, I don't know, I don't know"—but they're really in charge. He controls his family, controls his kids, controls his grandkids, controls the whole family, controls the church, but acts like, "I don't know, I don't know." But he did.

I saw him coming. There was nowhere to go. I shook hands with him and said, "How're you doing?"

He said, "I'm doing all right."

I didn't recognize him—I didn't recognize him. I said, "How's the church?"

He said, "Better than we've ever been."

"Really?"

And this is what he said: "God is at work in our church."

I've never heard him say anything like that; I've just heard him criticize. "God is at work in our church." I said, "That is wonderful."

He said, "We're in better shape spiritually and in every way than we've ever been in my memory."

"That is wonderful! Who is your minister?"

He said, "We have a woman." He never did give me her name. He said, "We have a woman."

I said, "You do?"

He said, "Yeah. I voted against her, and all my family voted against her, but we got outnumbered."

"And..."

He said, "I was wrong. I was wrong in my estimation of women." And then he looked at me and said, "Brother Fred, if I was wrong about her, I was probably wrong about a lot of other stuff."

Isn't that great? Finally, he met the gospel, broke the pattern, and he was making a new way.

✦

I was recently on a trip and was housed by my host in the Holiday Inn. It was there as it is everywhere, the place fills up quickly on Monday with businessmen who are traveling and earning their way. They come in with their suitcases and their little portable computers and whizbangs and all the other things that you have to take, and they're all frowning and scowling and pushing and shoving and gathering at night down at the bar, drinking and worrying about the state of things, trying to get ahead. I walked down the hall to my room, and there were three cleaning women out in the hall having a wonderful time. I said, "What's the matter with you women? Why aren't you working?" They were just laughing and having fun. I said, "What are you laughing about?"

And they said, "This is not for you—this is not for you!"

They were having so much fun. You know what they get paid? Minimum wage. Look at their faces, and look at the faces of the fellows down at the bar, "We're going to make it."

There's no connection. No connection.

A t Concourse A in the Atlanta airport, there's a big food court— maybe on some other concourses too—a big food court, all the fast-foods are around there, and you can go ahead and grab something and catch a plane. I had room in my calendar for a little breakfast. I had rushed down there to beat the traffic and now had to wait, so I went in there to find one that had something that was sort of breakfastlike. I finally found one, and it looked like breakfast, and I got a little something and a cup of coffee. I sat at a table in front of the place, and suddenly I heard singing, this marvelous male voice, deep and resonant and obviously well-trained. Singing. I noticed the song because it was "Lara's Theme" from *Dr. Zhivago,* which was played on a harp when our daughter Laura was married, and so I just like that song. And it was done so well. And then there was silence. I was about to finish my breakfast, and then that same voice again, "Come, Thou Fount of Every Blessing." Beautiful.

I went to the counter and said to the girl there, "Is that singing coming from over here?"

She said, "That's Albert, in the kitchen."

I said, "Can I speak to Albert?"

She said, "Well, yeah. Albert! Man out here wants to talk to you."

And out he came, this big, robust, smiling guy who said, "Yes, sir?"

I introduced myself; he introduced himself. "Albert," I said, "I want to thank you for the singing. It's marvelous."

He said, "You know what I'm doing, don't you?"

I said, "No. What are you doing?"

He said, "I'm auditioning."

"You're auditioning?"

He said, "Yeah, as many folks go through here all the time, there's bound to be one that's going to come along and going to take me out of this kitchen."

And then he went back, humming, into the kitchen, and I just thought, *There's not five percent of the population of Atlanta as happy as that guy in the kitchen.*

＊≡◎✦◎≡＊

On one of my trips some time ago, I don't know where, I arrived at the place where I was supposed to hold services on Friday evening, Saturday evening, and Sunday morning. When I pulled into the parking lot of the church, a funeral was concluding. People were moving to their automobiles; the hearse was still there. The minister saw me, recognized me, and motioned for me to come over. I didn't want to intrude; I was just waiting until it was over. He was standing next to the widow. He introduced her, he introduced me, and I felt awkward. I said to her, "This is no time for you to be meeting strangers. I'm sorry, and I'm really sorry about your loss." Her husband had been killed in a car wreck and left her with four children. I said, "I know this is a very difficult time for you."

She said, "It is. So I won't be at the services tonight, but I'll be there tomorrow night, and I'll be there Sunday morning."

I said, "Oh, you don't need to."

"Yes, I do."

I said, "Well, what I meant was, I know it's a very hard time."

And she said, "I know it's hard. It's already hard, but you see, this is my church, and they're going to see that my children and I are okay."

＊≡◎✦◎≡＊

When I was a boy, once I was taken out of the house and to the backyard and was allowed to lie on the grass and chew the tender stems of grass. You know how you do on a summer evening, just lie there, chew the tender grass, and look up at the sky. And my father said to me, "Son, how far can you think?"

I said, "What?"

He said, "How far can you think?"

"Well, I don't know what you mean."

"Just think as far as you can think up toward the stars."

I screwed my imagination down, and I said, "I'm thinking…I'm thinking…I'm thinking."

He said, "Think as far as you can think."

"I'm thinking as far as I can think."

He said, "Well, drive down a stake out there now. In your mind, drive down a stake. Have you driven down the stake? That's how far you can think."

I said, "Yes, sir."

He said, "Now what's on the other side of your stake?"

I said, "Well, there's more sky."

He said, "Move your stake."

And we spent the evening moving my stake out there. It was a crazy thing to do, but I will never thank him enough for doing it.

I had a student some years ago who, I'm sure, has since repented of his ways. First class in preaching, introduction to preaching, preaching in class, and I, that semester, allowed the students to choose their own texts. He chose Abraham offering Isaac. Well, first-year student, Abraham offering Isaac. I knew Martin Luther had said, "That text is too big, I can't preach on it," but my student, you know. So I called him into my office, and I said, "Are you sure you want to preach on this?"

"Oh yeah, I like that story. I want to preach on that."

I said, "Okay, but I think you'll discover this is a mountain too high, and you might not be able to climb it."

"Oh, I think I can do it."

"Okay."

So he explained Abraham offering Isaac, and then he needed an analogy. What was that like, to raise the knife over one's own son, in confidence that God will provide? So he said, "There are a lot of sacrifices we make, if we believe in God and want to serve God. I know when I came to school here, I arrived in early August to get settled, and my apartment wasn't ready, so I was put in temporary housing. It was not a very nice apartment, but the thing about it is, it was not air conditioned. And there I was in August, in Atlanta, without air conditioning."

So he knows what Abraham was all about.

When my sister Frieda, my only sister, was dying of cancer, I had gone back to visit and knew that the time there would be the last time I would see her. She asked me to help her prepare the funeral service, which I found extremely, extremely difficult to do. When we finished preparing the service, she asked me to pray, and this is what I did. I located myself, I located myself straight in front of the throne. Before I closed my eyes, I wanted to make sure I was in front of the throne, because what I wanted was God the throne, God the power, God the almighty. All things are possible with God.

When I had positioned myself straight in front of the throne, I bowed my head and prayed for her relief and for her healing as intensely and sincerely as I could, and I closed with Amen. I lifted my head, opened my eyes, and I was in front of the bleeding lamb. Now, who wants that? And she died.

There it is. God the power, God the one who identifies with us and suffers with us. You won't find a better picture in all the Bible than here.

First little church I served in Tennessee, the people were as poor as Job's turkey. Most of them got, you know, just a little pension of some sort from the Southern Railroad, and I fussed after them because they'd go into town and buy trinkets. From the pulpit I actually said sometimes, "You people need to buy beans and potatoes and some pork, and leave those trinkets and flower seeds and whatnot." Finally, Mrs. Glover got tired of it. She said, "Craddock, even the poor have a right to their pretties."

I think I was twenty years old when I read Albert Schweitzer's *Quest for the Historical Jesus.* I found his christology woefully lacking—more water than wine. I marked it up, wrote in the margins, raised questions of all kinds. And one day, one day I read in the Knoxville News-Sentinel that Albert Schweitzer was going to be in Cleveland, Ohio, to play the dedicatory concert for a big organ in a big church up there. According to the article he would remain afterward in the fellowship hall for conversation and refreshment.

I bought a Greyhound bus ticket and went to Cleveland. All the way up there I worked on this *Quest for the Historical Jesus.* I laid out my questions. I had my questions on a separate sheet of paper, but I made references to the pages. "You said…" because I figured, if there was conversation in the fellowship hall, there'd be room for a question or two.

I went there; I heard the concert; I rushed into the fellowship hall, got a seat in the front row, and waited with my lap of questions. After a while he came in, shaggy hair, big white mustache, stooped, and seventy-five years old. He had played a marvelous concert. You know he was master organist, medical doctor, philosopher, biblical scholar, lecturer, writer, everything. He came in with a cup of tea and some refreshments and stood in front of the group, and there I was, close. Dr. Schweitzer thanked everybody: "You've been very warm, hospitable to me. I thank you for it, and I wish I could stay longer among you, but I must go back to Africa. I must go back to Africa because my people are poor and diseased and hungry and dying, and I have to go. We have a medical station at Lambarene. If there's anyone here in this room who has the love of Jesus, would you be prompted by that love to go with me and help me?"

I looked down at my questions; they were so absolutely stupid. And I learned, again, what it means to be Christian and had hopes that I could be that someday.

When I went to my first little church, and the men were all wearing bibbed overalls, I went to the store and got some bibbed overalls. And I walked around there the first week saying to all the people, "I'm one of you!" Had plaid shirts and bibbed overalls. The second week I was there, some of the men loaded me into a '39 Dodge, drove to a nearby city, and had me measured for, of all things, a tailored suit. I loved it. "These are our clothes," they said, "not yours."

Up near me, at Fannin County Hospital, ministers around take turns being chaplain for the week. I took my turn, and the week I was on watch, there was a baby born. Not a lot born in that little bitty thirty-bed hospital. But I went there, it was about nine o'clock in the morning, and I saw all these people gathered, looking through the glass. There was that little bitty new baby, and it looked like a clan of people gathered around. I said, "What is it, boy or girl?"

"It's a girl."

"What's the name?"

"Elizabeth."

"Well, is the father over here in this group?"

"No." Looked back over there, and leaning against the wall, was a young man.

He said, "I'm the father."

I said, "Baby's name Elizabeth?"

"Yeah."

"Beautiful baby." She was squirming—you couldn't hear through the glass—but she was squirming, and red faced, and all like that. I thought maybe he might be concerned, and I said, "Now, she's not sick. It's good for babies to scream and do all that. It clears out their lungs and gets their voices going. It's all right."

He said, "Oh, I know she's not sick. But she's mad as hell." And then he said, "Pardon me, Reverend." I said, "That's all right. Why's she mad?"

He said, "Well, wouldn't you be mad? One minute you're with God in heaven and the next minute you're in Georgia."

Well! I thought, *Man, I've got myself a real mountain Gnostic here on my hands. This guy's been reading Plato.* I said, "You believe she was with God before she came here?"

He said, "Oh, yeah."

I said, "You think she'll remember?"

He said, "Well, that's up to her mother and me. It's up to the church. We've got to see that she remembers, 'cause if she forgets, she's a goner."

My sister Frieda died six years ago of cancer. She knew she was dying. About a week before she died, she had her husband label every item in the house that had been given to her over the last number of years, sometimes as much as twenty-five or thirty years ago. She had a wallhanging or a piece of glassware, or a vase or something, given by her friends, and she told him who gave her every item, and the occasion for it—birthday, anniversary, so forth.

Then he called these friends to come and get their presents to her. I was there that weekend when the people came driving up to receive the presents that they had given to Frieda, my sister, years ago. I was embarrassed about this, and when I got to the house, I had gone to spend the weekend with her, when I got to the house, a woman was coming out. She had driven from Huntsville, Alabama, and she had a vase that she had given my sister twenty-five years before. I said, "I want you to please forgive my sister. We were taught as kids you don't return gifts that people give you; you keep them and you prize them. But she is very ill, and I hope you'll understand that's the reason for it."

And the woman said, "I have never had a gift like this in my life—to have a gift that is twice blessed. For twenty-five years it reminded Frieda of me. Now it goes into my home and will remind me of her."

I listened once with Rabbi Silberman to a recording of a cantor reciting, reading large portions of the Hebrew Bible. My ear could not handle Hebrew so well—I could read it, but my ear wasn't good at it—but at a certain point, the cantor's voice broke and became very emotional. I asked the rabbi to stop the tape. I said, "The cantor became very emotional there, but I don't get it exactly, what was that?"

He said, "It was at the point where the text mentioned silver and gold."

I said, "Why the emotion?"

"The cantor is recalling the stealing of the silver and gold vessels from the temple."

Well, for me, silver and gold—I forgot the Hebrew there—but okay, silver and gold. But for the cantor, the voice quivered.

Some of you have heard me describe in detail a nine-pound sparrow walking down the street in front of my house, and I asked the sparrow, "Aren't you a little heavy?"

The sparrow said, "Yeah, that's why I'm out walking, trying to get some of this weight off."

And I said, "Why don't you fly?"

The sparrow looked at me like I was stupid and said, "Fly? I've never flown. I could get hurt!"

I said, "What's your name?"

And he said, "Church."

I recall not long ago, I was preaching at Ebenezer Baptist Church in Atlanta, Martin Luther King, Sr. and Jr.'s church. Joe Roberts, the pastor, had invited me. I was there to preach, and the service had moved to the point when I was to stand and speak. I'd moved to the pulpit, and I had my New Testament. They had asked me to read my own text, and I had turned to Mark 8 and was about ready to read, when Joe Roberts, who was seated up here along with several other persons, began to sing. Just as

I was going to say my first word, he started singing, "I feel much better now that I've laid my burden down," and then he sang some more. Then the associates started singing, and the musicians went to their instruments, the piano and the organ and the drums and the electric guitar, and the people started singing.

I'm standing there with Mark 8, waiting. Well, I suddenly realized, I'm the one up front, I'm the leader of this, so I started clapping my hands and singing. Then everybody stood up and started clapping their hands and swinging and singing, and it was just marvelous. Then at a certain point the pastor, Joe Roberts, put his hand out, it got quiet, they sat down, and I started preaching. I could've preached all day. Afterward I said to Joe, "Well, that kind of shocked me a little bit. You didn't tell me you were going to do that."

He said, "Well, I didn't plan to."

"Then why did you do it?"

And he said, "Well, when you stood up there, one of the associates leaned over to me and said, 'That boy's going to need help.'"

Years ago, near here in Los Angeles, the Society of Biblical Literature, scholars from all over the world, gathered and read papers to each other. I was present at the meeting. There were over three thousand scholars from many countries of the world. Between papers—and you can imagine the level of the papers, very detailed and working on little words and phrases and all of that; it took a lot of energy to listen to the papers—I went for a coffee break. I went down to the lobby of the hotel where we were meeting, and a woman, a plain-dressed woman, I would guess her to be forty, came up to me and said, "Are you attending the meeting here of Bible people?"

I said, "Yes."

She said, "Can anyone come?"

I said, "Well, to some of the sessions, yes."

"Well, I want to come."

I said, "Why?"

"I have walked the streets of Los Angeles since I was sixteen years old, selling myself. The other night I caught my daughter, a teenager, beginning the same life. I would like to be a Christian." She had a Bible, an old Bible with a zipper.

I couldn't think of a session for her to attend. I said, "Sit down," and we sat down and drank coffee, and I unzipped her Bible—it had not been unzipped I think—and read her some of it, and talked with her. We had a word of prayer. Then I went to a phone and called a church, and a minister came from that church, and they went away together.

There are people who would say, "See all the foolishness of those scholarly meetings? Anybody there probably couldn't even answer the woman's question, 'What must I do to be saved?' All that stuff is nothing. What they need is just somebody to answer the question."

My response to that is—phooey. That scholarly work is extremely important, otherwise the good ship Zion would be so covered with barnacles of prejudice and sentimentality it'd sink! But somebody's got to answer that woman's questions. In the church, you see, both the critical community and the confessing, evangelizing community are extremely important.

After the declaration of war by President Bush in what we called the Gulf War, some of us Christians in Atlanta had gathered for prayer. We had songs, we had scripture, we had prayer, and then songs, and scripture, and prayer. For a long time. There was seated next to me a young man, I think about seventeen or eighteen, might have been a freshman at the university, I don't know. In the course of the sentence prayers, he asked that God be with the women and the children in Iraq who would be hurt and killed in the war.

When it was over, a man in his mid-fifties came over to that young man and said, "Are you on Saddam's side?"

He said, "Uh, no sir."

"Well, you're praying for the wrong people."

When I was eighteen years old, a freshman at Johnson Bible College, I went down to a little church to preach near Rockwood, Tennessee. It was called Post Oak Springs, the oldest Christian church in Tennessee. There was a woman in that church whose husband had been a minister and had also taught at Lynchburg College years before. She was old, old, old, but she had me for lunch. Mrs. E. C. Wilson.

Mrs. Wilson said to me, "Now you want to remember, Mr. Craddock, that there will be a lot of times when you don't have anything to do. You'll be sitting in a waiting room, you'll be waiting on a bus, you'll be sick, you'll be somewhere with nothing to do. So what you want to do from the very first day is to remember some beautiful, short, complete statements of what you believe. Then when you're alone or afraid or in crisis or unable to decide, just call them up, and you can live on it." That's what she said, and that's what I did. And she was right.

I recall as a youngster, as a junior and senior in high school, going to summer conference at Bethany Hills near Nashville, Tennessee. That was the conference ground where the young people of Tennessee went. I remember the closing night, a consecration night. We gathered around the lake, and everybody held one of those little candles with a piece of cardboard so the tallow wouldn't drip down on your hand and make you say a bad word. There was a fire at the end of the lake, and there was the cross and a worship service. After the last song we were to go to the dormitories and not say a word until breakfast. It was a night of silence, of meditation, reflection. I remember that we sang all the stanzas of "Are Ye Able?" There were people in my junior year in high school, I remember, several young people went up and gave their lives to Christian ministry— we said, "full-time Christian service." It was already chewing on me; it was already working on me.

And I went to the dorm and lay on my cot, wide awake, couldn't sleep. What would it be like to give your life to the gospel? Are you able? To drink the cup? Are you able to be baptized with the baptism with which I am baptized? Are you able to give your life? Seems so wonderful. I had all those ideal images of what it would be like to give your life.

Some people quit because when they join, they notice they don't get any more attention. I said to this one woman in the parish, "Why don't you join this church? You're here every time, Sunday morning, Sunday evening, you come to Bible study, you come to Sunday school. Why don't you join?"

She said, "Well, I've noticed that after people join, they don't get much attention. I'd rather just stay a prospect."

There was a young minister in one of our churches in downtown Kansas City, years ago, and this church was not in a good location. It had sharply declined, but they had a service program for children of the inner city. There were games; there was food after school, games, food, Bible stories, and some singing. Forty-five, fifty, sixty children every day, games and food, fun, singing, Bible study.

A mother came and said to the young minister, "Are you the one running this program?"

"Yes, ma'am."

"My son's in this program."

"Well, we're glad to have him. We're having a good time. I hope he's having a good time."

"Well, he can play the games, and he can eat the food, but I don't want him listening to any of those stories."

"We just get them out of the Bible. They're just Bible stories."

"Well, I don't want him listening to any of those stories."

"Why? We're not trying to indoctrinate him. We're just telling Bible stories."

"He's gotten to where he's coming home now, thinking he's as good as anybody in Kansas City, and you're setting him up for bitter disappointment. I don't want him to hear those stories anymore."

And the young minister said, "I was trying to do good."

The young woman, twenty-eight years old, at St. Mark's church in Atlanta, said to me, "This is the first time I was ever in a church."

"Really?"

"Yeah."

"Well," I said, "How was it?"

She said, "Kind of scary."

I said, "Kind of scary?"

She said, "Yeah."

"Why?"

And she said, "It just seems so important." She said, "You know, I never go to anything important. This just seemed so important."

I remember upon the occasion of my mother's death—she had been kept as an invalid at my sister's home—we had gathered, the brothers and sisters, we were there, and she lay in state at the home. Friends and neighbors came, church members came, and it was a beautifully heavy time for us. There came running through the house a woman not of the family and not of the church, and she was telling us all how to interpret my mother's death. "Isn't it wonderful? Isn't it thrilling that Marie has gone to be with Jesus? No tears, no tears, isn't it wonderful?" She came up to me and said, "You're the one that's a preacher?"

I said, "Yeah."

"Then you're the one who really knows what a thrilling thing it is that she's no longer here, but…"

"Well, I wish she were here. In fact, I wish that she could make some biscuits again."

And I said to her, "If you think you're going to be making me feel guilty because I miss my mother, then you need to go to another house."

When Nettie and I finally got around to making a will, I think we were in our forties, maybe about fifty, we tried to tell our kids. They walked away. "We don't want to hear it." When we went to Ireland a couple of years ago, as is our custom when we go some distance and on the same plane, we reminded the kids where the lock box is and that it has a note inside saying, "Sorry."

So I called John, our son John, and he was not at home, but his wife Dee answered the phone. I said, "Dee, Nettie and I'll be leaving shortly now for Dublin, and I just wanted to remind you where the box was and the key."

And she said, "I don't want to listen to this. Y'all have a good time. I'm hanging up now."

You know how they feel.

Mattie Dixon didn't have a will; she hadn't taken care of anything. She was eighty-nine when she died. She didn't have any children; she was a widow, and she had some distant great-grandniece, nephews, cousins maybe. They didn't attend the funeral; they didn't really know her. They didn't know what to do, what would happen to the house, the property and the mementos, the personal effects. Finally, the taxes had to be paid; other bills had to be paid. The auctioneer came, and strangers crawled around all over the personal effects of Mattie Dixon. There was her wedding ring, one of those heavy ones. When she was alive, if you said to her, "Mattie, I love that ring, I'll give you a thousand dollars for it," she would turn that ring on her finger and say, "Fifty-six years of marriage, and you want to buy this? I wouldn't sell you this for ten million dollars!"

And the gavel of the auctioneer came down. "Sold. Two dollars."

I recall once, I was just a child, and I had a sickness. I had chilled in the night, and I was allowed to come and sleep on a pallet by the fireplace, the only fire in the house. While I was there not asleep I heard my mother and father talking in tones to guide the conversation away from me, but I heard it.

My father was telling this gruesome, painful story about a great-aunt of his that had died. They had no coroners. They'd get a doctor to sign a death certificate, but it would take several days for a doctor to come to this very remote, rural area. She'd died; surely she was dead, but her sister, my father's grandmother said, "I don't think she's dead. I really don't think she's dead. Don't bury her. Don't bury her. I don't think she's dead."

"But there's no…"

"Well, I don't think she's dead."

They went ahead. They had to bury her. Her sister just about went mad. Finally, she'd just woken up in the night screaming, and the menfolk went out and exhumed the body, opened the casket. The poor woman in the casket was turned to one side, and my great-grandmother went mad. The men said, "Well, it was in the way we took out the casket. It tilted, we almost…that's what did it. That's what did it."

And she said, "She wasn't dead."

I went in the fall, late fall, to speak at a church in Texas—well, it was a communitywide thing—and they sent me the plane ticket. I usually get my own, and they sent the plane ticket. It was first class. I'd never ridden in first class. When I got there, I chided them. I said, "You should not have spent the money on this. I'm not accustomed to this; you could've used the money for something else."

They said, "Well, there's a couple in the church that have a craft shop, and they go to Hong Kong a lot to buy things. They have a bunch of frequent flier miles, and they said, "Why not just use it to get the preacher over here?" And so they did, and I was up in first class. I was trying to figure out how to behave up there, so I got out my long yellow tablet and my pencil to do some work as I usually do on the plane, hoping that I was doing the first-class sort of thing, and I looked around. There were twelve seats in first class. The eleven others, all men, had laptops and had cell phones to their ears, and I looked down at my tablet and thought, *Fred, you've had it. You know, it's all over for you.*

When I was growing up—I use that expression in a generous sense—on the farm in western Tennessee, our closest neighbor and good neighbor was a black family named Graves, John and Jeanetta Graves, just wonderful, wonderful people. She was the happiest person, the most loving person I knew. She laughed as though it came from her whole body, and she loved everybody—she had long arms and embraced everybody.

She became pregnant, had a son, and she was pleased to say to the world, "This is going to be a child of reconciliation," because in rural west Tennessee in those days there was still some racial prejudice. There was still some Civil War talk. So she said, "My boy is going to be a child of reconciliation," and she named him Lee Grant. Think about it.

My mother said, "That was a mistake Jeanetta. Nobody's going to like him now."

Jeanetta said, "Oh no, no, he's going to be the end of all this hostility and hatred. He's going to be the child of reconciliation."

When he went to town once, he let me go along, and I have never witnessed one person suffering the verbal abuse that he suffered from people who didn't know him. He was a very gracious, good man, but his name was Lee Grant. And Jeanetta, his mother, said to me, "I don't think you ought to go to town with Lee Grant anymore—you might be hurt."

I already was hurt. Strange.

I have a brother, retired. He's older than I, and he picks up trash along the highway. I said, "What do people say to you?"

He said, "Well, some people think that I'm demented. Some think that I have been given community service by a judge. Some think I am a prisoner, working on the side of the road."

"Well, then, why do you do it?"

And he said, "I can't stand for things to be so trashy." Out there picking up other people's garbage. Strange.

A man down the road from us when I was a boy was named Cook, Mr. Cook. I never knew his first name; he was Mr. Cook. We said "Mr." and "Mrs." to everybody. Mr. Cook was a hateful man, and he killed our dog. Our dog was named Dempsey after the prizefighter Jack Dempsey. He was just a dog, but he was our dog, and he went with us everywhere. And Mr. Cook killed him.

When our father came in one evening before dinner, I said to him, "Mr. Cook killed Dempsey." My father didn't even stay in the house for supper. He went down the road, and the five of us kids were saying, "Go get him, go get him." My mother was in the kitchen, crying and praying. Father was gone a long time, and my mother was very worried. When Daddy came back in, he had blood on his shirt. We wanted to know what happened. He said, "I never knew that Mr. Cook was an epileptic."

"What? He's an epileptic?"

"I went down there to let him have it, and he was on the porch in a seizure—chewing his tongue, and his mouth was bleeding. I got my hand in his mouth, got him free of chewing his tongue, and took him in the house and cared for him until he was able to get up and sit in a chair. That's where I got the blood."

I said, "Well, now that he's feeling better, you going to go down there now and beat him up?"

And he said, "No." That seems strange; he killed Dempsey.

Ministers as a lot are strange. I learned it quite early, at summer camp at Bethany Hills. I went every year. I liked summer camp—beautiful place, good friends, and a lot of playing and eating and having fun. There was a minister there—first minister I really ever was around—his name was Frank Drowota. He was from England and still had a drag in his voice after all those years. He was the pastor of Woodmont Christian Church in Nashville, and he was one of the teachers, counselors, whatever they were called, at summer youth camp.

I remember one evening after we left the dining hall, he walked along with me and said, "Can I talk to you?"

"What'd I do wrong?"

He said, "Have you ever considered becoming a minister?"

I said, "No sir, never, never have." I was seventeen, about to begin my senior year in high school, and he ruined everything for me. What a thing to lay on a kid. All I wanted to do was go where the girls were, save some money to get a car, go to school some more, someday get married, have a house, a garden, and two weeks of vacation in the summer. What else is there? And then he lays that on me. I thought about it when I got up in the morning; I thought about it when I went to bed at night.

I am still thinking about it. He was a minister, and he did that.

Rear Admiral Thornton Miller came into my life in younger years. I was a freshman at Johnson Bible College, and Rear Admiral Miller came and spoke in chapel and then talked to some of us boys after chapel. He was the highest ranking chaplain in the military at the time. He looked great in that uniform. He had been at Normandy on that June day of the slaughter, and he described it that evening in the dorm to some of us, of going from soldier to soldier, screaming, crying, dying, trying to say a few words of comfort, have prayer, words of comfort, have prayer.

Someone asked, "Up and down the beach, with the shells going everywhere? Why did you do that?"

His answer: "I'm a minister."

And the person began again, "But didn't you ask if they were Catholic or Protestant or Jew? Did you just…I mean, if you're a minister…"

Now, get this. Rear Admiral Miller said, "If you're a minister, the only question you ask is, 'Can I help you?'"

That's really strange.

I met someone coming out of an antique shop in Blue Ridge, North Georgia. The town has become just antique stores. That's all we have. This minister came out. I knew he was a minister; he had a clerical collar, and he had an old box under his arm. I said, "You bought something in there?"

He said, "Yeah."

I said, "What'd you get?"

He said, "I found in there, right at the end of an old washbasin and a churn, this box. And I got the box and the contents for a dollar."

I said, "What's in it?" He opened it up, and it was full of old words. A box full of words, burned or notched in wood. He pulled out one, and it said, "Til death do us part." He pulled out another one, and it said, "I'll follow you wherever you go." Pulled out another one, it said, "I give you my word," all this kind of stuff.

I said, "What are you going to do with that?"

He said, "The reason the man let me have it for a dollar is, he said, nobody talks that way anymore. They're useless." This minister thought they were great, but then you know how ministers are. They're strange.

Couple of years ago, I went back to the community where I was born and reared and went to public school, in west Tennessee. On Sunday evening while I was there, I went with a friend to his church, a small church, not many there, but I noticed they had new leaded glass windows, beautiful windows and, I calculated, expensive windows. While I wondered how they could afford it, I began to read the names, the dedications in the windows. I didn't recognize any of the names, and I was reared there. I said to my friend, "Are these new people who have come in? I don't understand this; I don't recognize any of these strange names."

He said, "No, a church in St. Louis ordered these windows from Italy, and when they got them, they didn't fit. They advertised in a church paper that they would sell them because they were going to have new ones made. They were so cheap we bought them."

And I said, "Well, they sure are beautiful, but what are you going to do about the plaques?"

He said, "Well, the board discussed that, and we decided to leave those names up there. It's good for us in our little church to realize that there are some Christian people besides us."

Have you ever been present when anybody unjoined the church? I experienced that only once. It was in Oklahoma, and my wife and I belonged to a church, it was a rather large church there. One Sunday morning during the closing hymn, a hymn of dedication, consecration, a woman in her mid-thirties, we both knew her, went to the front. People stopped singing and were looking at each other. Why's she doing that? She's already a member. Maybe she's going to rededicate her life. Maybe she's going to become a minister. So we all hushed and waited.

She spoke quietly to the minister; we didn't know what she was saying. At the conclusion of the hymn, he asked us all to sit down. We waited as she turned around to address us. What she said in essence was, "I owe it to you to let you know that I am leaving the church. I am not joining another church. I am leaving the church. And since I made public notice when I came, I wanted to make public notice as I leave. I don't think it's right just to drift off into inactive membership. I am leaving the Christian circle. I have been disappointed. What I expected from the church and from the gospel and from the scriptures and from God, I have not received. I am leaving. For those of you who have expressed concern about my life"—and hers was a very troubled life—"for those among you who know it and have expressed concern about it, I thank you. To that extent, I have some regret. Thank you."

It was a strange morning. We didn't know how to leave. We didn't pay attention to the benediction. We bumped into the furniture and into each other leaving. And many of us spent Sunday afternoon thinking about what she did. It made us determine whether we would claim our own commitment in view of the fact that one of our group had decided to leave.

Our neighbor, bless her heart, she sometimes is five feet tall, but not usually. She's in her sixties. Her husband's a farmer; he comes in at uneven times. She had supper ready, had it in the oven waiting for him. She was in the living room doing needlework. She looked up from her crocheting, whatever it was, and saw a face, the burly, ugly face of a strange man looking in the window. She put the needlework down and went over to the door, and she pushed the piano across the door. When her husband came in, he got the neighbor, and they pushed it back.

And she says, "Every once in a while, he looks up at me at the breakfast table and says, 'Who helped you move that piano?'" Nobody did. She had to move it.

Some years ago, in my Oklahoma days, I preached a meeting of several night services in an oil field near Kiefer, Oklahoma. Now in those days, we're talking years ago, at least in that place, some of the wells were all run by one big engine at a house, a pump house I call it. I don't know what the oil people call it. A pump house and a great big engine, ch-ch-ch, ch-ch-ch. There was a man that lived with his family near that engine house, pump house, to take care of it, oil it, take care, make sure it kept going, and rods went out from that to several wells.

My host and hostess for that time of revival lived in the pump house, right there. They were very gracious people and had a nice guest room. I went in there and went to bed. Next to me, right outside the window, was ch-ch-ch, ch-ch-ch, ch-ch-ch. I just was elevated different numbers of inches from the mattress. I never did really sink into the bed. The next day my hostess said, "Well, did you have a nice evening? Did you sleep well?"

"Well, no, no I didn't."

"Well, what was the matter?"

I said, "The pump!"

And she said, "Oh, I forgot about the pump. We never hear the pump until it stops."

I went to a little rural church once to speak. They had a real terrible rainstorm. They canceled the service, and everybody knew it because they had those telephones. But I didn't have one of those telephones, and I didn't know it. So there I drove from Enid, Oklahoma, out to there, slipping and sliding on those roads—dirt, mud, a little gravel. Two of the men had thought about the fact that the preacher wouldn't know that they were not having it, so they went to the church to wait for me, to tell me there was no service. When I went in, they were seated at the table that had on the front of it "In Remembrance of Me," and they were playing cards. I said, "What in the world are you doing?"

They said, "Well, we're just playing a little poker, waiting for you to come."

I said, "On that table?"

One of them said, "Well, a table's a table's a table."

And I said, "No it isn't." No it isn't. Not for me.

Once, before I preached in Oklahoma City at a church, a woman came up just before I stood up to speak; she came right up to the pulpit and said, "Before you talk, I need to know something."

I said, "Yes, ma'am?"

She said, "Are you a knocked-down, killed in the Spirit, washed-clean, picked-up, Spirit-filled charismatic Christian?"

I said, "Well, I'm a Christian."

"Well, that's not what I asked you."

And I said, "Well, what did you ask me?"

"Are you a charismatic?"

I said, "Yes, ma'am, I am."

She was real pleased and smiled big and said, "What's your gift?"

I said, "Teaching."

And she said, "Oh," and she left. I didn't think it was all that bad.

When I taught in Oklahoma, there was a man that was concerned about improving the quality of preaching in the churches. Well, aren't we all? But he had a lot of money, and the president of our little school—we were hanging by our financial fingernails—said, "I believe he's going to give some money for the preaching program." Well, I taught preaching. He said, "I'd like for you to go with me to talk to him." We made several visits; they call it cultivation. The guy had a lot of money. Finally, the president called me and said, "He's going to make a gift, a sizable gift. You want to go along?"

"Oh yeah, I'd love to be there." Well, I went with the president; we went by car. Drove over there to the man's office. He was ready for us. Had stuff out on his desk.

He said, "Before we finish this, I think we ought to pray."

Oh yeah, I had a prayer; but we didn't pray, and the president didn't pray. The man prayed himself. He had the money, he had the prayer, he had the whole thing. He had the prayer. "Amen."

"Amen." He took his pen and started to sign his name. The lawyer apparently had fixed everything out, we're talking big gift here. He took his pen, and just before he put his name down he looked up and said, "Now, this all goes for the preaching program?"

"Yes sir, that's what it goes for."

He started to write. He said, "Now, you do understand, none of this goes for women or blacks?"

The president stood up, I stood up, and the president said, "I'm sorry, we cannot accept your money under those conditions." We started to leave.

The man said, "Well, there are plenty of schools that will."

I wanted to stay and talk about it a little bit, but it was all over. We were silent all the way home. That man had given to schools and churches over sixty million dollars, but not a penny is to go to the women or the blacks, you understand?

My now-deceased friend Oswald Goulter, thirty years a missionary to China, was under house arrest for three years. He would be released by the Communists if he promised to go home. He said he would come home. He wired back, the missionary society sent him money for his transportation, and he took a ship. He went down to India to catch a ship, and when he was in the coastal city in India before leaving, he heard that there were a lot of Jews sleeping in the barn lofts in that city. They'd been denied entrance to every country in the world except that one, and they had gone inland and were living in barn lofts. It was Christmas time. Oswald Goulter went around to those barns and said to the Jews, "It's Christmas! Merry Christmas!"

They said, "We're Jews."

He said, "I know, but it's Christmas!"

They said, "We don't observe Christmas. We're not followers of Christ. We're Jews."

He said, "I know, but what would you like for Christmas?"

"We don't keep Christmas."

"I know, but what would you like? If somebody gave you something for Christmas, what would you like?"

They said, "Well, we'd like some good German pastry."

"Good!" So he went looking, and he finally found some German pastry at some shop there in that city. After cashing his passage check, he took boxes of German pastries to these Jews and said, "Merry Christmas!" Then he wired the missionary society and said, "I need a ticket home."

When that story was being told, there was a young seminarian sitting in the front row, and he was absolutely incensed. He said to Dr. Goulter, "Why did you do that? They don't believe in Jesus!" And Dr. Goulter said, "But I do. I do."

I was recently on my side of Atlanta at the Delta flight counter trying to get some travel plans changed. It was all confused, so I went over to that little substation on Saturday morning to get it straightened out. The young woman, an agent, was waiting on me, and while I was waiting for her to get it cleared up, a man came in and was being attended to by the agent beside her. He was next to me, a middle-aged man, distinguished looking, even though he had on his Saturday morning jogging suit. I was waiting and I was waiting and finally I heard the young woman say to him, "Now, sir, when do you plan to go to Seattle?"

He said, "Uh, uh, uh, uuuhhh, just a minute," and he ran out to the car, came back, and gave her the date.

She worked it into the machine, and then in a few moments she said, "And, uh, sir, when do you plan to return?".

He said, "Uuuuuhhhh, just a minute," and he ran out to the car, came back, and gave her the date. He said, "I know it doesn't seem like I do any traveling, but actually I travel a lot. The fact is, Friday afternoon at 5, I turn my brain off. I turn my brain back on Monday morning at 9."

"I know how you feel." But then she said, "Sir, don't you go to church?"

He said, "Yeah, I go to church, but you don't have to turn on your brain to go to church." I could've kicked him. But there was something true about it.

This woman that I'm thinking about was in her sixties when she told me. She said it happened when she was about seven. Her mother and father were always real chatty at supper. It was a large family, a lot of kids, and suppertime—I call it supper, some people call it dinner—but at suppertime they just all had a good time, everybody laughing and talking, what happened, and what was good, and what was bad, and this and that, Mom and Dad talking, the kids all talking. It was just a wonderful time.

"Just before supper, Mom and Dad got into it," she said. "I'd never seen them like that. I'd never heard them talk to each other that way—their faces red and screaming at each other. Then they saw us kids waiting for supper, and they got quiet. Momma said, 'Sit down. Let's eat.' We sat down, and it was quiet as a graveyard. Nobody talked during supper. Nobody talked at breakfast. Nobody talked at lunch. Nobody…"

She said for three weeks nobody spoke at a meal, and Mom and Dad did not speak. "After about three weeks, they began to be civil to each other, but our home was never the same."

I was once, years ago, going out to San Diego, and I was on that side of the plane that just has two seats. You know, some of the planes have three seats on one side, two on the other. I was on the side with two seats, on the aisle, and this woman, looked to be in her forties, was at the window. I spoke to her. I usually work on the plane, read, study, read a paper, whatever, but I noticed she was crying, noticeably crying. And, you know, being a minister and all, you're supposed to say something. So I said, "I see this is not a very happy trip for you." See, I'm very perceptive.

She said, "No, it isn't."

"Well, I'm sorry."

She said, "I'm going to my father's funeral."

"Oh, well, I'm sorry." She kept crying.

What else could I say? "I can tell by your tears that you and your father were very close."

And she said, "No. On the contrary, I haven't spoken to my father, written to my father, called my father, seen my father, in seventeen years. Seventeen years."

"Really?"

"In fact," she said, "the last time I saw him I was in his home, and we got into a quarrel. I left the table, threw my napkin in my plate, and as I slammed the door leaving his house, I said, 'You can go to hell.' That's the last thing I said to my father. And now he's dead."

One of my students was going away. He preaches out from Atlanta, has a church of about, on a good Sunday, thirty, thirty-five. He said, "Uh, Prof, would you preach for me Sunday? I'm going to be out of town." He was going to Aspen, Colorado, to do the Lord's work.

And I said, "Well, yeah, I'm free. Where is it?"

He told me where it was, out on a dirt road, great big cemetery and little frame building. It's just a one-room building. And he said, "Now, they expect the preacher always to teach the Sunday school class."

I said, "Which class?"

"There's only one class. We have a class in the sanctuary, little opening exercise, they sit there and have Bible study, then they get up and clear their throats and scratch and walk around and come back in, and then it's worship."

I said, "Sure. What are you studying?" I thought maybe they were on the standard uniform lessons.

He said, "No, we're just finishing Matthew's gospel."

I said, "Well, where are you?"

"Matthew 28:16–20, the great commission."

I said, "Well, I can handle that."

I got there. For the class there were about twenty, the average age, oh I don't know, 117 or something like that. I mean, these are old people. There isn't a younger person anywhere within sight of the church at all. I said, "Well, the minister tells me you're at the end of Matthew, Matthew 28:16–20."

"Yeah, that's right."

"Everybody have your Bibles open?" They have the Living Bible, Good News, RSV, King James, New King James, New International, all kinds. That's not intimidating, that's exciting. "How does yours have it?"

"Really? It has that?"

"Yeah, what does yours say?"

"Well mine says so-and-so. You think that's the same?" Pretty soon they're all, you know, into it.

Well, I said, "Let's read it first. Now the eleven disciples went to Galilee, to the mountain to which Jesus had directed them. When they saw him they worshiped him, but some doubted. And Jesus came and said to them, 'All authority on heaven and on earth is given to me,'" and so forth. One of the men sitting there, I could tell he was a farmer, he was brown as gingerbread except for a white scalp, he said, "Well I'll be dogged."

I said, "What's the matter?"

He said, "I never noticed that before."

"What'd you notice?"

He said, "That's kind of strange."

I said, "What's strange?"

"The way that's put there."

I said, "Well, what's strange?"

"'When they saw him, they worshiped him, but some doubted.' And then the next verse says, 'And Jesus came and said to them.' Looks to me like he's already there."

That's true, isn't it? They saw him and worshiped him, and the next verse says, "and Jesus came." And that man said, "I'll be dogged."

I said, "That is kind of awkward, isn't it?"

And he said, "Sure is."

I said, "How do you explain that?"

He said, "Well, I don't know. Maybe Matthew's sort of like me, couldn't write too good." A woman on the end of the pew down there said, "You don't talk that way about the Holy Scriptures," and he never did, he didn't say anything else the whole time. And neither did she.

I asked her, and she said, "Well, there are just a lot of things we don't understand, but we'll understand by and by." She had the biggest Bible of all, but she wasn't going to touch it.

"Anybody else have a theory?"

It was kind of quiet, and then a woman spoke up and said, "Sometimes when I write my daughter at night, I get tired and sleepy, so I just quit and finish up the next morning. I know sometimes I even change pens from the one I used at night, and the next morning it's not even in the same color ink. I know it doesn't tie up too good, so maybe Matthew wrote part of that at night, and the next morning he finished it up."

Hey, now that's pretty good. I mean, you spend $29.95 for books that tell you that, you know?

So we talked about it and finally one said, "Well, I don't know why it's that way, but I know starting there at 18, that just all goes together right through the end. 'And Jesus came and said to them, All authority…' That just all goes together."

I said, "Sure it does. In fact, there's a German New Testament scholar, considered the greatest New Testament scholar in the last seventy-five years, named Bultmann that agrees with you."

And she said, "Really?"

"Yeah." Boy, she was thrilled. She and Bultmann had that stuff cold. I went on and explained what he said. And she agreed, that's right, he just said it in a different way, but that's right. I took that occasion then to elaborate that you have three of these in Matthew, Jesus coming to his disciples. At the Mount of Transfiguration, and Jesus came to them. Walking on the water, and Jesus came to them. And this one. Every one of them, they're afraid and they worship him. It's sort of like a risen Christ story. Even walking on the water—they thought it was a ghost. I said, "These are all called epiphany stories, Jesus coming to the church," and we talked about it. Now those people had no education, but good minds. The student in that church had said to me at least a thousand times, "Well, Prof, this is all right here in the classroom, but out at my church this stuff won't fly."

Phooey. That's the Greek word for it. Phooey. Now, if you get a little education and try to come down through the chimney, nobody wants it. But if you share it pastorally and listen to people, they can handle it.

I'll never forget that Sunday at Columbia, Tennessee, Central Avenue Church. Some kids were at the water fountain between Sunday school and church, between Sunday school and worship. "Well, what'd you kids study this morning?" They had their big Sunday school pictures with the memory verse, you know, and there was Jesus and the woman at the well, the memory verse about the living water. I said, "That's what I'm going to preach on today, and they've already had it." I mean, I was like a wrinkled prune, I thought, *Boy, they stole my thunder; what am I going to do?* I was all frustrated during the worship, because there are those kids, and this is old hat to them. So I tried to disguise it and, you know, make it seem new. When the fact was, those kids were the best listeners, nudging each other. They were better listeners than their parents because they knew it, and the parents didn't know what I was talking about. See? And that's when I learned, if you teach it and then preach it, the preaching is much more powerful.

I was in a church gathering in Ponca City, Oklahoma, and somebody asked me during the question-and-answer period what I thought about somebody's view of the Bible that had just been published and they had all read about. I discussed it, and I said, "There's a lot of thought there, and I'm sure this is a very sincere person, but his view of the Bible is not adequate for me. I just think he puts too much water in the wine."

Afterward a woman came up to me and gave me two tickets to the state Women's Christian Temperance Union banquet. She wanted my wife and me to go, and I said, "But why this?"

And she said, "We just don't have enough ministers speaking out against drink, and I appreciated what you said." Now, what did I say, and what did she hear?

When I was a kid, I went to church with my mother, and the minister would speak to my mother, "How're you, Miz Craddock?" and the five of us kids would go along like little ducks along after our mother. "How're you, sonny? How're you, honey? How're you, sonny? How're you, honey?"

But I remember when another minister came to our church, and about his fifth or sixth Sunday when I went along there, he said, "Fred, how're you doing?" He was the best minister that ever was at that church, because there's a big difference between "sonny" and "Fred."

I recall as recently as, I don't know, eight years ago, I was preaching at a church in Atlanta, and following the service the minister was taking me to lunch. He said, "Let me pick up a bit." You know, ministers do all of it, picking up bulletins and straightening around and all. And I began to pick up some bulletins in the back of the sanctuary, waiting on the minister.

I picked up one, and over on the side where the announcements were, in the little blank space at the bottom—it was a real busy church, so they made all their announcements in less than a half page—there was writing. In one handwriting it said, "Shall we close the deal today?" And a different handwriting said, "But it's Sunday." And in the first handwriting underneath that, "But if we don't close it today, we may lose it."

And it reminded me, not everybody sits in rapt attention, all the time. You think you're up there proclaiming the eternal verities, and somebody back there is working a deal.

One of the best sermons I heard from one of my students was by a young woman who didn't have a church, no place to preach. So she went over to Wesley Woods, little place there for elderly people, three levels of care, you know those places, and they let her have a Sunday afternoon service once a month in the sunroom. People would wheel down there and listen to her. She was a sprightly young woman, and she said to me, "Would you come and hear me preach and evaluate my preaching? I want to be a good preacher, and I don't have a church."

I said, "Okay, okay," and I went one Sunday afternoon. She read her text from Luke 18, the mothers bringing the babies to Jesus. Permit the little children to come to me. I said, "Great day in the morning! Of all the texts to read here—the average age is 117—and she reads, 'Bring the little children'?"

This is what she did. She said, "I still can't get over the fact that Jesus' helpers, the twelve apostles, ministers, the clergy, said, 'Get the children out of here.' In a way, I can understand this. I mean, after all, they make noise. They have to be cared for. Sometimes you have to get up and leave with them. They take everybody else's time. Besides that, they can't give anything; they can't teach a class; they can't sing in the choir. They're just, you know, they're a burden. I understand that." She went through all that. "But Jesus said, 'Leave them alone, let them come.' That's kingdom people."

And those old people just nodded—"That's right, that's right." She never mentioned elderly people, and they perceived. It's marvelous.

I was walking one afternoon, and I passed a corner where a man was doing something that fascinated me, and I stopped my walk and watched him. He had a pile of bricks, and the thing he was doing was measuring each brick—how long it was, how wide it was, how deep it was. He'd throw a bunch of good-looking bricks out. He said, "I've got to get them all exactly the same."

I said, "Why?"

He said, "I'm building a church, and I want it to stand."

See, there are people who think that the way to really have a church is to get people that are from the same economic and social and educational background, then they'll all be together. Boy, he started stacking those bricks; they were all just alike. I went by the next afternoon, and they were all just piles of brick. Fell down.

I went on around the corner, and I saw a man with a pile of rocks. You've never seen such a mess in your life—no two of them alike, round ones, dark ones, small ones, big ones, and little ones. I said, "What in the world are you doing?"

He said, "I'm building a church."

I said, "You're nuts! The guy down there had them all alike, and he couldn't make it stand!"

He said, "This'll stand, this'll stand."

"It won't either."

"Yes it will."

I said, "You can't get it to stand. The fellow down there had them all…"

He said, "It'll stand."

And he went over to a wood tray, took something like a hoe, and began to stir something back and forth. Looked a lot like cement to me, but that's not what he called it. He put healthy doses of that between the stones. I went back thirty-four years later, and it was still there. It was that stuff in between, looked a lot like cement. That's not what he called it. You know what he called it.

Some years ago, one of the, if not *the,* best students I had in preaching finished seminary having had a number of courses in preaching, excelling in all of them, and preaching in the school chapel with extraordinary ability. He went to the first church, somewhere in Texas, a small town. The first Sunday came for the first sermon, and he didn't show up. They sang all the stanzas of all the hymns selected. Still no preacher. Then there was worry, and they began to go looking in the parsonage and everywhere. The wife joined in the search, but they couldn't find the preacher.

Finally, out in the little park in that town, sitting on a picnic table, there was the preacher thumping pebbles. His wife fussed a bit at him. The members of the board gathered and said, "We understand, nervousness, first Sunday, and all like that. However, you will get over your nervousness by next Sunday."

And so the next Sunday he did appear in the pulpit. He wrote me a note, "1:15 p.m., First Sunday, First Church. Today I dropped a stone in the water. Whether there will be ripples, whether they will reach the shore, remains to be seen. In appreciation…" Signed his name.

He had such a lofty view of preaching that he was paralyzed.

Last December I was summoned to Superior Court, DeKalb County, Georgia, to serve on the jury. On Monday morning at 9:00, 240 of us formed the pool out of which the juries for civil and criminal cases would be chosen. The deputy clerk with the Superior Court stood and called the roll. Two hundred and forty names. She did not have them in alphabetical order; you had to listen.

And while I was waiting, I began to listen. There were two Bill Johnsons, one was black and one was white, and they were both Bill Johnson. There was a man named Clark, a Mr. Clark, who answered when the clerk read, "Mrs. Clark."

He said, "Here."

She looked up and said, "Mrs. Clark."

And he said, "Here."

She said, "*Mrs.* Clark."

And he stood up and said, "Well, I thought the letter was for me, and I opened it."

She said, "We summoned *Mrs.* Clark."

"Well, I'm here. Can't I do it? She doesn't have any interest in this sort of thing."

And the clerk said, "Mr. Clark, how do you know? She doesn't even know she's been summoned."

This roll call is pretty good. There was a man there whose name I wrote down phonetically because I couldn't spell it. His name was Zerfeld Leischenstein. Zerfeld Leischenstein. I remember it because they went over it five or six times, mispronouncing it. He insisted it be pronounced correctly, and finally stood in a huff and said, "I see no reason why I should serve on a jury in a court that can't pronounce my name."

The woman next to me said, "Leischenstein? I wonder if he's a Jew?"

I said, "Well, I don't know. Could be. Does it matter?"

She said, "I am German. My name is Zoeller."

And I said, "Well, it doesn't matter, that was forty years ago."

"He and I could be seated next to each other in a jury."

I said, "Well, you were probably just a child when all of that happened years ago."

And she said, "I was ten years old. I visited Grandmother. She lived about four miles from Buchenwald, and I smelled the odor." Calling the roll.

W hen my wife and I finished our service at the student church when I was in seminary, our last Sunday there they gave us a gift. It was a quilt some of the women of the church had made, and they stitched into the top of the quilt the names of all the church members. Every time we moved and we'd come across that quilt, we'd spread it out on the bed, and we'd start remembering. We'd remember something about everyone... "There's Chester, who voted against and persuaded the others to vote against my raise. There's Mary and John, who put new tires on our car. There's Lloyd, very quiet, never said anything. There is his wife Marie. There is that marvelous woman Lois who lived with that man who drank and became violent, yet she was always faithful and pleasant, and he was dying with cancer when we went. My first funeral there, you remember." And this is the way we go over the quilt. Don't call it a list.

I remember when they brought the famous list to Atlanta. The workers set it up in the public place—block after block to form a long wall of names, Vietnam names. Some of us looked at it like it was a list of names; others went over closer. Some walked slowly down the columns. There was a woman who went up and put her finger on a name, and she held a child up and put the child's hand on the name. There was a woman there who kissed the wall at a name. There were flowers lying beneath the wall.

Don't call it a list. It's not a list.

B efore I married and served in the little mission in the Appalachians, I moved down to a place on Watts Bar Lake, between Chattanooga and Knoxville, a little village. It was the custom in that church at Easter to have a baptismal service. My church immerses, and it was held, this baptismal service, in Watts Bar Lake on Easter evening at sundown. Now out on the sandbar, I, with the candidates for baptism, moved into the water, and then they moved across to the shore where the little congregation was gathered, singing around a fire and cooking supper. They had constructed little booths for changing clothes with hanging blankets. As the candidates moved from the water, they went in and changed clothes and went to the fire in the center. Finally, last of all, I went over, changed clothes, and went to the fire.

Once we were all around the fire, this was the ritual of that tradition. Glenn Hickey, always Glenn, introduced the new people, gave their names, where they lived, and their work. Then the rest of us formed a circle around them, while they stayed warm at the fire. The ritual was that each person in the circle then gave her or his name, and said this, "My name is…, and if you ever need somebody to do washing and ironing…" "My name is…If you ever need anybody to chop wood…" "My name is…If you ever need anybody to baby-sit…" "My name is…If you ever need anybody to repair your house…" "My name is…If you ever need anybody to sit with the sick…" "My name is…, and if you ever need a car to go to town…" and around the circle.

Then we ate, and we had a square dance. And then at a time they knew, I didn't know, Percy Miller, with thumbs in his bibbed overalls, would stand up and say, "Time to go," and everybody left. He lingered behind and, with his big shoe, kicked sand over the dying fire. And my first experience of that, he saw me standing there still, and he looked at me and said, "Craddock, folks don't ever get any closer than this."

In that little community, they have a name for that. I've heard it in other communities too. In that community, their name for that is "church." They call that "church."

Do you have a piece of paper? Do you have a piece…Well, use your worship bulletin. Would you write in the margin somewhere or at the bottom these words: *I thank my God for all my remembrance of you.* I thank my God for all my remembrance of you. And write a name. You choose the name. You remember the name. Write another name, and another name, and another name.

Have you written any names? Do you have a name or two? Keep the list. Keep the list, because to you, it's not a list. In fact, the next time you move, keep that. Even if you have to leave your car, and your library, and your furniture, and your typewriter, and everything else, keep that with you.

In fact, when your ministry has ended and you leave the earth, take it with you. I know, I know, I know. When you get to the gate, St. Peter's going to say, "Now look, you went into the world with nothing, you've got to come out of it with nothing. Now what've you got?"

And you'll say, "Well, it's just some names."

"Well, let me see it."

"Well, now, it's just some names of folks I worked with and folks who helped me."

"Well, let me see it."

"This is just a group of people that, if it weren't for them, I'd have never made it."

He'll say, "I want to see it." And you'll give it to him, and he'll smile and say, "I know all of them. In fact, on my way here to the gate I passed a group. They were painting a great big sign to hang over the street. And it said, 'Welcome Home.'"

In the fall of the year, even after the days grow short and the air crisp, I still go out on the patio alone at the close of the day. It usually takes only a few minutes to knit up the unraveled sleeve, quietly fold it, and put it away. But those few minutes are necessary; everyone needs a time and a place for such things.

But this particular evening was different. I sat there remembering, trying to understand the painful distance between the day as I had planned it and the day as it had been. The growing darkness was seeping into mind and heart, and it was at night. Looking back on it, I know now that it was this evening on which the Idea came to me, but frankly I was in no mood to entertain it.

It was not really a new Idea, but neither was it old. It was just an Idea, and it returned the next evening. I was relaxed enough to play with it a little while before it went away. The following evening I spent more time playing with the Idea and feeding it. Needless to say, I grew attached to the Idea before long. Then I had the fear that it belonged to one of the neighbors and that I would not be able to keep it. I went to each of the neighbors, "Is this your Idea?"

"No, it isn't our Idea."

I claimed it for myself and exercised an owner's prerogative by giving it a name. I named it Doxology.

I took Doxology inside to our family supper table. Supper is family time, and conversation is usually reflection upon the day. If all are unusually quiet, I often ask, "What was the worst thing that happened today?"

John answers, "The school bell rang at 8:30."

"Well, what was the best thing that happened?"

"It rang again at 3:30."

Tongues are loosed and all of us—Laura, John, Nettie, and I—share our days. Supper is a good time and pleasant, and the whole family agreed that Doxology belonged at our table.

The next day Doxology went with me downtown for some routine errands, but somehow they did not seem so routine. We laughed at a child losing a race with an ice cream cone, his busy tongue unable to stop the flow down to his elbow. We studied the face of a tramp staring into a jewelry store window and wondered if he were remembering or hoping for better days. We spoke to the banker, standing with thumbs in his vest before a large plate glass window, grinning as one in possession of the keys of the kingdom. We were delighted by women shoppers clutching bundles and their skirts at blustery corners. It was good to have Doxology along.

But I had to make a stop at St. Mary's Hospital to see Betty. Betty was dying with cancer, and the gravity of my visit prompted me to leave Doxology in the car. Doxology insisted on going in and was not at all convinced by my reasons for considering it inappropriate to take Doxology into the room of a dying patient. I locked Doxology in the car.

Betty was awake and glad to see me. I awkwardly skirted the subject of death.

"It's all right," she said. "I know, and I have worked it through. God has blessed me with a wonderful family, good friends, and much happiness. I am grateful. I do not want to die, but I am not bitter." Before I left, it was she who had the prayer.

Back at the car, Doxology asked, "Should I have been there?"

"Yes. I'm sorry I did not understand."

Of course, Doxology went with the family on vacation. This summer we went to the beach down on the Gulf. What a good time! A swim before breakfast, a snooze in the afternoon sun, and a walk on the beach for shells in the evening. Doxology enjoyed watching the young people in dune buggies whizzing by and spinning sand over on the man half-buried beside his wife, turning herself in the sun like a chicken being barbecued. It was fun to walk out into the waves. These waves would start toward us, high, angry, and threatening, but as they drew near they began to giggle and fall down. By the time they reached us, they had rolled over, so we scratched their soft undersides, and they ran laughing back out to sea.

There is no question: Doxology belongs on a vacation.

Too soon it is school time again. I return to seminary classes.

It was from the class on Romans that I was called to the phone. My oldest brother had just died, heart attack. When stunned and hurt, I get real busy to avoid thought. Call the wife. Get the kids out of school. Arrange for a colleague to take my classes. Cancel a speaking engagement.

And, oh yes, stop the milk, the paper, the mail, and have someone feed the dog. Who can take my Sunday school class? Service the car. "I think I packed the clothes we need," the wife said, as we threw luggage and our bodies into the car.

All night we drove, across two states, eyes pasted open against the windshield. Conversation was spasmodic, consisting of taking turns asking the same questions over and over. No one pretended to have the answers. When we drew near the town and the house, I searched my mind for a word, a first word to the widow. He was my brother, but he was her husband. I was still searching when we pulled into the driveway. She came out to meet us, and as I opened the car door, still without that word, she broke the silence: "I hope you brought Doxology."

Doxology? No, I had not. I had not even thought of Doxology since the phone call. But the truth is now clear: If we ever lose our Doxology, we might as well be dead.

Have you ever listened to a sermon in which the lineup of illustrations were Albert Schweitzer, Mother Teresa, and missionaries who had their feet frozen off in the tundra of the north? As a young person sitting in church listening to those stories with a few Napoleon stories thrown in, I just sat there swinging my legs over the pew, as I still do, and said to myself, *It's a shame you can't be a Christian in this little town. Nobody is chasing or imprisoning or killing Christians.*

Then I went away to summer camp to Bethany Hills, an inspiring time, a night of consecration around the lake, and candlelight, and just everything about it so moving. We sang, "Are Ye Able?" I went back to the dorm and lay on my bunk and said to God, "I'm able." "Are you able to give your life?" "I'll give my life," and I pictured myself running in front of a train and rescuing a child, swimming out and getting someone who was drowning.

I pictured myself against a gray wall and some soldier saying, "One last chance to deny Christ and live." I confessed my faith, and they said, "Ready, aim, fire." The body slumped, the flag was at half mast, and widows were weeping in the afternoon. Later a monument is built, and people come with their cameras. "Johnny, you stand over there where Fred gave his life. Let's get your picture."

I was sincere then, as I have been these forty-five years since. "I give my life," but nobody warned me that I could not write one big check. I've had to write forty-five years of little checks: 87 cents, 21 cents, a dollar three cents. Just nibbled away at this giving of life.

Nettie and I had returned from Oklahoma to one of our favorite vacation spots, The Great Smoky Mountains. We were at dinner in a restaurant out from Gatlinburg near the small community of Cosby. We were in a rather new restaurant called the Black Bear Inn. It was very attractive and had an excellent view of the mountains.

Early in the meal an elderly man approached our table and said, "Good evening." I said, "Good evening."

He said, "Are you on vacation?"

I said, "Yes," but under my breath I was saying, *It's really none of your business.*

"Where are you from?" he asked.

"We're from Oklahoma."

"What do you do in Oklahoma?"

Under my breath but almost audible, I was saying, *Leave us alone. We're on vacation, and we don't know who you are.* I said, "I am a Christian minister."

He said, "What church?"

I said, "The Christian Church."

He paused a moment and said, "I owe a great deal to a minister of the Christian church," and he pulled out a chair and sat down.

I said, "Yes, have a seat." I tried to make it seem like I sincerely meant it, but I didn't. Who is this person?

He said, "I grew up in these mountains. My mother was not married, and the whole community knew it. I was what was called an illegitimate child. In those days that was a shame, and I was ashamed. The reproach that fell on her, of course, fell also on me. When I went into town with her, I could see people staring at me, making guesses as to who was my father. At school the children said ugly things to me, and so I stayed to myself during recess, and I ate my lunch alone.

"In my early teens I began to attend a little church back in the mountains called Laurel Springs Christian Church. It had a minister who was both attractive and frightening. He had a chiseled face and a heavy beard and a deep voice. I went to hear him preach. I don't know exactly why, but it did something for me. However, I was afraid that I was not welcome since I was, as they put it, a bastard. So I would go just in time for the sermon, and when it was over I would move out because I was afraid that someone would say, 'What's a boy like you doing in a church?'

"One Sunday some people queued up in the aisle before I could get out, and I was stopped. Before I could make my way through the group, I felt a hand on my shoulder, a heavy hand. It was that minister. I cut my eyes around and caught a glimpse of his beard and his chin, and I knew who it was. I trembled in fear. He turned his face around so he could see mine and seemed to be staring for a little while. I knew what he was doing. He was going to make a guess as to who my father was. A moment later he said, 'Well, boy, you're a child of…' and he paused there. And I knew it was coming. I knew I would have my feelings hurt. I knew I would not go back again. He said, 'Boy, you're a child of God. I see a striking resemblance, boy.' Then he swatted me on the bottom and said, 'Now, you go claim your inheritance.' I left the building a different person. In fact, that was really the beginning of my life."

I was so moved by the story I had to ask him, "What's your name?"

He said, "Ben Hooper."

I recalled, though vaguely, my own father talking when I was just a child about how the people of Tennessee had twice elected as governor a bastard, Ben Hooper.